ENCYCLOPEDIA

ANIMALS

Dragonfly nymphs are ferocious hunters, often feeding on young fish and tadpoles.

The nymphs grow and moult over many years before climbing onto a reed or rock to emerge as an adult.

◀ Blue dasher dragonflies are also called blue pirates. Females are rarely as blue as the males, which only turn blue as they mature. These dragonflies live in North America and into Mexico.

DID YOU KNOW?
Dragonflies can reach speeds of 58 km/h to escape from birds.

Mantids

- **A mantid is a carnivorous insect** that has a long, thin body and legs. It holds its front legs up and together.

- **These insects** are also known as mantises.

- **They live in warm** and tropical places where there are plenty of plants.

- **Mantids attack other animals** including arthropods, amphibians and reptiles.

- **Their front legs** are long, spiked and strong. They use them to grab prey. The spines help them to grip onto slippery animals.

- **The eyes are large** and spaced apart. This helps a mantid to not only see its prey but to judge its distance so it can strike with speed and accuracy.

- **There are two groups** of mantids: flower mantids and praying mantids. Flower mantids are often colourful so they blend in with the plants on which they live.

- **Female mantids** sometimes eat males after mating with them, or even during mating. Males can continue to mate even when they have had their heads bitten off.

▼ A mantid has forward-facing eyes, which gives it binocular vision. This means that it can use the images from both eyes to accurately work out how far away its prey is.

Devil's flower mantids are green and white and they grow leaf-like shields on their backs as a form of camouflage.

When they are startled, mantids raise their front legs to display bright colours, or spread their wings to warn off predators.

Praying mantises are usually green so their prey cannot see them lurking on a plant. They have long necks and can turn their heads right round behind them.

Most praying mantises are 2–10 cm long, but giant specimens measuring more than 15 cm have been found.

Stick insects

- **Stick insects** are the longest insects in the world and Chan's megastick insects measure more than 50 cm long with their legs stretched out.

- **Females are usually** bigger than males. Some types have wings.

- **A stick insect has a** long, stick-like body so it can feed on plants without being spotted by predators such as birds and reptiles.

- **They live in warm places**, especially tropical forests, where they most easily blend in with twigs and sticks.

- **When a stick insect** is scared it might make a foul smell, a loud noise or flash its wings. If a predator grabs a leg, the stick insect can shed it and grow a new one.

- **A female lays** up to 1200 eggs at a time. They can produce young even without mating with a male, which means the young are all copies of their mother.

- **When a stick insect** is on a plant it usually stays completely still, so it cannot be seen. Sometimes, stick insects rock from side to side but the reason for this is not known.

- **Leaf insects** are similar to stick insects. Their flat green or brown bodies so closely resemble leaves that they can be almost impossible to see when hiding on a plant.

- **While some leaf insects** look like fresh, green leaves, others are wrinkled and brown like a dead leaf.

- **Both leaf and stick** insects are often bred as pets, although they do not usually live for more than a year.

◀ Stick and leaf insects belong to a group of insects called phasmids. There are about 2500 species including this spiny leaf insect, which is also known as Macleay's spectre. Most phasmids are nocturnal, eat plants and have incomplete metamorphoses.

Grasshoppers and crickets

◀ Most grasshoppers are smaller than 8 cm long and are camouflaged to hide among plants. They have much shorter antennae than crickets.

- **The 25,000 species** of grasshoppers, crickets and katydids are most common in warm parts of the world.

- **Most grasshoppers** and locusts feed only on plants, but many other members of this family feed on both animals and plants.

- **Powerful back legs** allow grasshoppers and crickets to jump huge distances.

- **Some grasshoppers** can cover up to one metre in a single leap. This helps them to escape from predators.

- **Grasshoppers sing** by rubbing their hind legs across their closed forewings. Crickets sing by rubbing rough patches on their wings together.

- **Grasshoppers have ears** on the side of the abdomen, while crickets have ears on the knees of their front legs.

- **Crickets chirrup** faster the warmer it is.

- **If you count** the number of chirrups a snowy tree cricket gives in 15 seconds, then add 40, you get the approximate temperature in degrees Fahrenheit.

- **Locusts are grasshoppers** that sometimes form vast swarms that can include millions of individuals. They can devastate huge areas of crops when they land to feed.

- **Katydids are named** for their song, which sounds like 'katy-did, katy-did'. Their ears are on their front legs, like crickets.

▼ *The spines on a thorny devil katydid's body deter predators. Other species flash bright colours, or rely on camouflage to stay out of sight.*

DID YOU KNOW?

Foam grasshoppers produce toxic foam that covers their body. They take the toxins from plants that they eat.

Bees and wasps

- **Bees and wasps** are narrow-waisted insects with four transparent wings. They usually have hairy bodies.

- **There are over** 20,000 species of bee. Many, such as leaf-cutter bees, live alone but over 500 species, such as honeybees, live in colonies.

- **Worker bees collect nectar** and pollen from flowers.

- **Wasps do not make honey** but adults feed on sweet food, such as fruit, plant sap and nectar.

- **Female ichneumon wasps** lay their eggs inside caterpillars and other insect grubs. When the eggs hatch, the young wasps have a supply of living food to help them grow and develop.

- **Spider-hunting wasps** attack and paralyze spiders with their venom.

- **The tarantula hawk wasp** lays its eggs in tarantula spiders and grows to 8 cm. It has a painful sting.

- **Sawflies are close relatives** of bees and wasps with striped abdomens. They don't sting, but they do attack crops, especially fruit, so they are regarded as pests.

- **Some bumblebees** live in colonies, like honeybees. They make nests using grass and usually build them at ground level, or in the soil.

- **Fig wasps lay their eggs** inside figs, which have tiny flowers inside. As they travel between fig trees, the female pollinates the flowers so that fig seeds can grow.

▶ Wasps build hexagonal cells in their nests. Each cell contains an egg or a growing grub. The adults take care of the brood.

Honeybees

Honeybees live in hives. The inside of the hive is a honeycomb made up of hundreds of six-sided cells.

A honeybee colony has a queen (the female bee that lays the eggs), tens of thousands of female worker bees, and a few hundred male drones.

A worker bee visits about 2000 flowers every day. To make 100 g of honey, the worker has to visit about 200,000 flowers full of nectar.

Honeybees tell each other where to find flowers rich in pollen or nectar by flying in a dance-like pattern.

▼ A honeybee carries pollen on its legs, in special pollen baskets. It will perform a 'waggle dance' to tell its hive-mates where to find good flowers.

◄ *When animals all move together they are sometimes described as a swarm. Bees often swarm when they are on the hunt for a new nesting site, and thousands of worker bees follow their queen.*

🐾 **Honeybees originally lived** in Europe and Asia but were taken to the Americas to help fertilize crops and for their honey and wax.

🐾 **African killer bees** were bred by scientists by crossing honey bees and African bees. They are more aggressive than other bees and sometimes form large, angry swarms.

🐾 **Bees that just feed** on rhododendrons and azaleas (types of flowering plants) produce honey that is strong in toxic chemicals from the plants. Humans who eat the honey can be poisoned by it.

🐾 **Female honeybees** beat their wings to move air around the hive.

363

Ants

- **Ants are a vast group** of insects related to bees and wasps. Most ants have a tiny waist, long, jointed antennae and are wingless.

- **They are the main insects** in tropical forests, living in colonies of anything from 20 to millions of individuals.

- **Ant colonies** are mostly female. One or more queens lay the eggs, which are fertilized by males called drones. Female ants do all the work in the colony, including defending the nest and caring for the eggs.

- **Ants that protect** the nest are called soldiers. They have bigger jaws, for fighting, than other ants.

- **Wood ants squirt acid** from their abdomen to kill their enemies.

- **Army ants march** in huge swarms, eating small creatures they meet.

▼ Leafcutter ants feed on fungus, which they grow in underground farms. They cut leaves and carry them back to the farm, where they are used to grow the fungus.

- **Groups of army ants** cut any large prey they catch into pieces, which they carry back to the nest. Army ants can carry 50 times their own weight.

- **Ants known as slavemakers** raid the nests of other ants and steal their young to raise as slaves.

- **Honeypot ants** have special workers that store sugary liquid in their abdomens. In a drought, they release the sugary food to other workers in the nest.

- **Tropical weaver ants** use silk produced in the jaws of their own grubs to sew leaves together and make a nest.

Toxic invertebrates

▼ Velvet ants are not really ants at all, but wingless wasps with such a nasty sting that they are called 'cow killers'.

- **Invertebrates use poisons** to kill or paralyze their prey or to defend themselves from their own predators.

- **Invertebrates such as spiders**, wasps and scorpions produce poisons inside their bodies. Insects such as caterpillars, grasshoppers and beetles often get their poisons from the plants they eat.

- **Most poisonous insects** are brightly coloured – including many caterpillars, wasps and cardinal beetles – to warn off potential enemies.

- **The stings of bees and wasps** are at the back of their bodies. Bumblebees and wasps can sting repeatedly. A honeybee can only sting once because its sting has a barbed tip, and some of its organs are pulled out when it flies off.

- **Some invertebrates** are not toxic, but they pretend to be. Hoverflies, for example, have black and yellow stripes to mimic the warning colours of wasps and bees.

- **Ladybirds make** nasty chemicals in their knees.

- **When attacked**, swallowtail caterpillars may hit their attacker with a smelly forked gland from a pocket behind their head.

- **Centipedes inject poison** into their prey with their claws. Giant centipedes can kill animals as big as mice.

- **Scorpions have sharp stings** at the end of their tails, linked to sacs of poison. They can control how much poison they inject. Large scorpions use their poison mainly for defence, and use their big pincers for killing prey.

Index

Index

Page numbers in **bold** refer to main subject entries; page numbers in *italics* refer to illustrations.

D

E

F

Acknowledgements

All artwork from the Miles Kelly Artwork Bank

The publishers would like to thank the following sources for the use of their photographs:

t = top, b = bottom, l = left, r = right, c = centre, bg = background

Front cover: Suzi Eszterhas/Minden Pictures/FLPA
Back cover: (t) Pei Chung Davy/Shutterstock.com, (c) Pal Teravagimov/Shutterstock.com,
(b) Sebastian Knight/Shutterstock.com

Alamy 23 Steve Bloom Images

Ardea 86 Nick Gordon

Corbis 36 Pete Oxford/Minden Pictures; 46 Flip de Nooyer/Minden Pictures; 94 DLILLC;
148 Tim Davis; 176–177 Marco Simoni/JAI

FLPA 38 Jurgen & Christine Sohns; 42 J.-L. Klein and M.-L. Hubert; 43 Michael & Patricia
Fogden/Minden Pictures; 63 J.-L. Klein and M.-L. Hubert; 266 Reinhard Dirscherl;
270 Richard Herrmann/Minden Pictures; 272 Yva Momatiuk & John Eastcott/Minden Pictures;
288 Reinhard Dirscherl; 291 Birgitte Wilms/Minden Pictures; 326 Ingo Arndt/Minden Pictures

iStockphoto 15 Snowleopard1; 362 & 363 arlindo71

National Geographic Creative 128 Flip/Minden Pictures

NaturePL 33 Dietmar Nill; 131 Brandon Cole; 214 Franco Banfi; 224 Pete Oxford;
262 Alex Mustard; 263 MYN/Seth Patterson; 302 Alex Mustard/2020VISION;
305 Jeff Rotman;

Photoshot 249 NHPA

Shutterstock 1 Galyna Andrushko; 3 Marina Jay; 5(t) Tony Campbell, (b) behtesham;
6(t) Tony Campbell, (b) Eric Isselee; 7(t), (b) Robert Eastman; 8(t) cristi180884, (b) cbpix;
9(t) irin-k, (b) Alex Staroseltsev; 10–11 niall dunne; 12(bl) Eduard Kyslynskyy, (br) Ethan
Daniels; 13(bl) DonLand, (br) Chantal de Bruijne; 14 Sari ONeal; 16 Tom Reichner; 17 Arend
van der Walt; 18 Serge Vero; 19 Manamana; 21 Norma Cornes; 24 Wayne Lynch/All Canada
Photos/Corbis; 26 Eric Gevaert; 27 Rich Carey; 29 rlandin; 30–31 Justin Black; 32–135,
370–383 (top banner) treesak; 37 worldswildlifewonders; 39 BMJ; 40 Eric Isselee; 41 Eric
Isselee; 47 Ultrashock; 48 Jiri Balek; 49 Geoffrey Kuchera; 50 Stacey Ann Alberts; 55 Hung
Chung Chih; 57 outdoorsman; 58 Daniel Hebert; 60 Erwin Niemand; 61 mylifeiscamp;
62 Danny Alvarez; 64 Riaan van den Berg; 66 Eduard Kyslynskyy; 68 Dennis W. Donohue;
69 Stuart G Porter; 70 milosk50; 71 Dennis W. Donohue; 72 Stuart G Porter; 74 Graham
Taylor; 77 amphaiwan; 81 Neil Burton; 88 S.Cooper Digital; 92 Anna Kucherova; 98 erwinf;

104–105 wolfso; 107 Johan Swanepoel; 108 EcoPrint; 110 Neil Burton; 111 Schlegelfotos; 113 Henri Faure; 114 Zhukov Oleg; 116 Pyty; 118–119 Mark Bridger; 120 Johan Swanepoel; 121 Mogens Trolle; 122–123 Victor Shova; 124 Andrea Izzotti; 127 Jordan Tan; 132–133 Krzysztof Odziomek; 135 Jorg Hackemann; 136-193(top banner) Super Prin; 136–137 Tania Thomson; 138 Arto Hakola; 140 TravisPhotoWorks; 141 Danny Alvarez; 142 FloridaStock; 144l Aaron Amat, (r) phugunfire; 145 Anan Kaewkhammul; 146 Andrew Burgess; 147 Dmytro Pylypenko; 149 Footage.Pro; 150 Stubblefield Photography; 151 Fredy Thuerig; 152 BMJ; 155 Sergei Kolesnikov; 154 Marco Barone; 156 Erni; 157 Braam Collins; 158 Anna Omelchenko; 162 Nazzu; 163 Nagel Photography; 164–165 Vladimir Kogan Michael; 166–167 Steve Collender; 168 Iakov Filimonov; 169 Nick Fox; 170 Critterbiz; 172 Bildagentur Zoonar GmbH; 173 Tom Reichner; 175 Jarry; 178 francesco de marco; 179 feathercollector; 180 Lovely Bird; 181 Panu Ruangjan; 183 feathercollector; 184 HTU; 186 hfuchs; 187 Jeremy Reddington; 189 Sebastian Knight; 191 Vetapi; 193 Eric Isselee; 193 PeterPhoto123; 194–229(top banner) Enrique Ramos; 194 Natursports; 197 Joe Farah; 198–199 Janelle Lugge; 201 apiguide; 202–203 larus; 207 Webitect; 208 Audrey Snider-Bell; 209 scubaluna; 210 fivespots; 212 Vishnevskiy Vasily; 215 cellistk; 216 Eric Isselee; 219 Andre Coetzer; 220 Stephen Mcsweeny; 221 Eric Isselee; 222 Achimdiver; 223 poeticpenguin; 227 Sergey Uryadnikov; 228 Meister Photos; 230–243(top banner) Eric Isselee; 230–231 Brandon Alms; 233 Steve Bower; 234 Dirk Ercken; 235 bogdan ionescu; 237 Eric Isselee; 239 Vittorio Ricci; 241 Johan Larson; 242; 243 Dirk Ercken; 244 Levent Konuk; 246 Matt9122; 247 Joshua Francis; 251 stockpix4u; 252 Targn Pleiades; 253 Rich Carey; 254 A Cotton Photo; 258 fish1715; 261 Amanda Nicholls; 265 Kletr; 269 Richard Whitcombe; 275 Rich Carey; 276 JonMilnes; 279 Circumnavigation; 281 Ethan Daniels; 283 Matt9122; 284 Mogens Trolle; 286 Radka Palenikova; 289 Alex Staroseltsev; 290 Dusty Cline; 292 Joe Belanger; 293 Pawe? Borówka; 295 Vilainecrevette; 296 Amanda Nicholls; 298–299 Rich Carey; 307 littlesam; 308 Sphinx Wang; 310 Jiang Hongyan; 311 Lightboxx; 314 Alexandra Lande; 315 Lia Caldas; 316 Ethan Daniels; 317 Beverly Speed; 318–319 blewisphotography; 321 wacpan; 322 Tomatito; 323 Dreamframer; 325 skydie; 331 Cosmin Manci; 332 Aleksey Stemmer; 334 smuay; 335 Tony Bowler; 336 Pan Xunbin; 337 Sarin Kunthong; 339 Kletr; 341 vblinov; 342 NH; 344 Tsekhmister; 345 Nick Stubbs; 346 Ksenia Ragozina; 350 krisgillam; 352 Bonnie Taylor Barry; 354 M.Khebra; 356 Andrew Burgess; 358 Jiang Hongyan; 359 Dr. Morley Read; 361 Csati; 363 StevenRussellSmithPhotos; 368 Johan Swanepoel

All other photographs are from:
Digital Stock, digitalvision, ImageState, John Foxx, PhotoAlto, PhotoDisc, PhotoEssentials, PhotoPro, Stockbyte

MINI

ENCYCLOPEDIA

ANIMALS

Author
Camilla de le Bédoyère

Miles
KeLLy

First published in 2015 by Miles Kelly Publishing Ltd
Harding's Barn, Bardfield End Green, Thaxted, Essex, CM6 3PX

2 4 6 8 10 9 7 5 3 1

Publishing Director Belinda Gallagher
Creative Director Jo Cowan
Editorial Director Rosie Neave
Senior Editor Claire Philip
Designer Simon Lee
Image Manager Liberty Newton
Indexer Eleanor Holme
Production Elizabeth Collins, Caroline Kelly
Reprographics Stephan Davis, Jennifer Cozens, Thom Allaway
Contributors John Farndon, Steve Parker, Barbara Taylor

ISBN: 978-1-78209-789-1

Printed in China

British Library Cataloguing-in-Publication Data
A catalogue record for this book is available from the British Library

Made with paper from a sustainable forest

www.mileskelly.net
info@mileskelly.net

Contents

 ## How animals live

 ## Mammals

 Birds

Reptiles

Amphibians

Fish

Invertebrates

Habitats

🐾 **An animal's home** is called its habitat. Across the world, there are many types and sizes of habitat.

🐾 **Each habitat** needs to provide the animals that live there with food, water, shelter and protection from predators.

🐾 **Grasslands are vast** habitats that are home to many herbivores (plant eaters) such as rhinos, elephants, antelope, horses, rabbits and termites.

🐾 **Life for animals** that live in a desert habitat is challenging because water, essential to life on Earth, is in scarce supply.

🐾 **Few animals** have a permanent home in the frozen Arctic and Antarctic, due to the extreme cold.

🐾 **Arctic ground squirrels** cope with freezing temperatures by hibernating (going into a deep sleep) for up to eight months of the year.

🐾 **Within a large habitat** there are often smaller habitats. For example, in rainforests a huge variety of plants provide many homes for animals to live in.

- 🐾 **The world's oceans** are all connected to each other. They are the largest single habitat on Earth.

- 🐾 **Oceans provide** an enormous number of habitats, from the deep sea to the coasts where waves crash against rocky shores.

- 🐾 **Freshwater habitats** include lakes, ponds, pools and rivers.

- 🐾 **Many animals** – such as frogs – are able to spend part of their lives in fresh water, and part on land. Some animals can move between fresh water and the sea.

- 🐾 **Humans have created** a new habitat: towns and cities. Many animals now live alongside humans in urban areas.

▼ *There are countless numbers of habitats across the world, but nine main types are recognized: deserts, grasslands, coniferous forests, temperate forests, tropical forests, mountains, polar regions, fresh water and oceans. They provide homes for about 9 million types (species) of animals.*

Senses

🐾 **In order to survive**, an animal needs to know what is happening in the world around it. It uses its senses to get this information.

🐾 **The five main senses are**: sight, hearing, smell, touch and taste.

🐾 **The senses gather information**, which is sent to the animal's brain. The brain sends instructions to tell the animal to react in a certain way, such as running from danger.

🐾 **Even simple animals** without brains have senses and are able to react to a change in their environment.

🐾 **Some animals**, such as sharks, are able to sense the electricity given off by another animal's muscles.

🐾 **Blood-sucking mosquitoes** can detect carbon dioxide – the gas that humans breathe out – which guides them to their victims.

🐾 **Bats and toothed whales** locate their prey using a special sonar sense, or echolocation. They use sound waves to build up a picture of their prey's location, its size and the direction in which it is moving.

◀ *A monarch butterfly has two large compound eyes, each made up of thousands of tiny lenses. It tastes and smells through holes found all over its body, but especially on its super-sensitive antennae.*

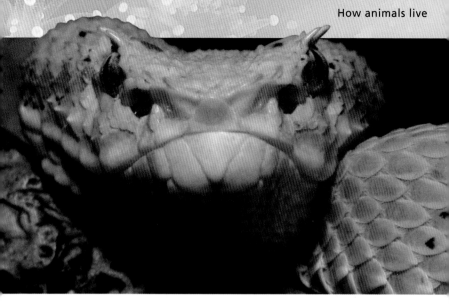

▲ *Pit-viper snakes, such as this eyelash pit viper, are able to sense the heat given off by another animal's body. This sense is so acute they can even calculate how far away their prey is. Like most other pit vipers, the eyelash pit viper hunts at night.*

- **Dung beetles look up** at the stars to help them walk in a straight line when they are rolling balls of dung back to their dens.

- **Insects can't see** the colour red.

- **Falcons are birds of prey** with great eyesight. They can see a mouse up to 1.5 km away.

- **Spiders' legs are covered** with little hairs that can smell and taste. Similarly, butterflies can taste with their feet.

- **Fish have a line** of special sense cells that run along their bodies, called a lateral line. It senses movement in the water, warning fish if a predator is nearby.

Movement

◄ *A rufous hummingbird can beat its wings an astonishing 52–62 times per second.*

- **Few plants can move**, but most animals are able to travel from one place to another. Their main reasons for moving are: to find food, to find mates, to avoid being eaten and to find shelter.

- **Vertebrates move** with the help of a skeleton and muscles. The places where bones connect are called joints.

- **Animals have evolved** many different ways of moving from place to place, from crawling and scampering to swimming, running, flying and gliding.

- **Gibbons are apes** of Southeast Asia. They have extremely long arms and hands that they use to grab onto branches as they swing through trees.

- **Sifakas are Madagascan lemurs** that leap along the ground, taking big steps and spreading their arms out for balance.

- **A hummingbird can hover** and suck nectar at the same time by moving its wings in a figure of eight pattern.

🐾 **Moving fast is helpful** when it comes to catching prey, or escaping from an attacker, but it takes a lot of energy.

🐾 **Quick-movers**, such as cheetahs and some desert spiders, run the risk of moving so fast that they overheat and die.

🐾 **Flying squirrels can't actually fly**, but they can use the large flaps of skin between their arms and legs to glide to the ground.

🐾 **Swifts are among** the most impressive of all flying birds. They have tiny feet and rarely come to land – they even sleep while they are flying.

🐾 **Some animals go on long journeys** in search of food, mates, or good places to breed. These journeys are called migrations.

▶ African wildebeest and zebras take part in one of the world's longest migrations on land. Up to 1.5 million wildebeest travel 2900 km in search of food and water.

17

Nutrition

- **Nutrition is the term** for what animals eat and how they get their food.

- **Plants can make** their own food using sunlight, carbon dioxide and water. Animals, however, must eat in order to get energy.

- **Carnivores eat other animals**. Usually they have to hunt, catch and kill those animals, so most carnivores are predators too.

- **A scavenger** is an animal that eats any food it finds.

- **Some scavengers** eat the dead bodies (carrion) of other animals that have either died naturally, or have been left by a predator. These animals, such as vultures, are called carrion-feeders.

- **A herbivore is an animal** that eat plants, such as a hippopotamus or a hare.

DID YOU KNOW?
In one day, a blue whale can eat the weight of an elephant in food, but it can also go for weeks without eating at all.

▼ *Hippos do not have a high-energy lifestyle so they can eat a small amount of food for such large animals. They eat grass and mostly graze at night.*

▶ Grizzly bears that live near salmon rivers grow bigger and stronger than other brown bears. Their fishy diet is packed with muscle-building protein.

🐾 **Herbivores often** have large stomachs and long guts because plant material is difficult to digest.

🐾 **Omnivores are animals** that eat a range of foods, including plants and animals. For example, humans, pigs and brown bears are omnivores.

🐾 **Carnivores need sharp** slicing teeth for cutting meat while herbivores need big, broad teeth for grinding tough plants.

🐾 **Birds have a gizzard** – a special organ for grinding up food as it passes through the body. Some birds have stones or grit in the stomach to mash it into smaller pieces.

🐾 **Merriam's kangaroo rats** live in deserts and never need to drink. They get all the water they need from the seeds they eat.

🐾 **While some animals**, such as sharks and crocodiles, may survive for many weeks without a meal others – such as shrews – must eat every few hours.

Reproduction

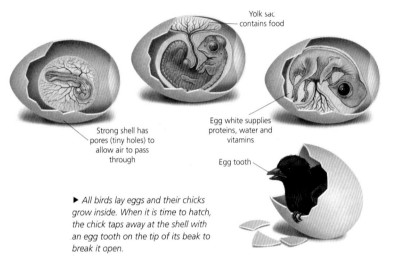

Yolk sac contains food

Egg white supplies proteins, water and vitamins

Strong shell has pores (tiny holes) to allow air to pass through

Egg tooth

▶ *All birds lay eggs and their chicks grow inside. When it is time to hatch, the chick taps away at the shell with an egg tooth on the tip of its beak to break it open.*

- **The way that an animal** makes its young is called reproduction.

- **Some small animals**, such as coral polyps, can reproduce simply by growing an exact copy of themselves.

- **Many animals** need a mate to reproduce. In order to attract a mate they enact certain behaviours, known as courtship.

- **Male frogs** croak loudly to attract mates when it is time to breed, and many birds sing to each other.

- **Male birds of paradise** perform incredible dances and show off their beautiful feathers to females to impress them. Females are fussy about which male they will mate with.

- **Male walruses** are much larger than females. They need to be massive to survive the ferocious battles they have with one another in order to win the right to reproduce.

- **Most animals begin life** as a small egg. Most insects, amphibians, reptiles, snakes and birds lay eggs that then develop outside their parents' bodies. The egg contains food for the growing animal.

- **Some parents produce thousands** – even millions – of eggs which they abandon. Only a tiny number of the eggs are likely to grow into adults.

- **Most mammals** keep their young inside their bodies while they grow. They invest so much time and energy into their young that mammals usually have far fewer young than other animals.

▲ A baby elephant develops inside a protective sac of liquid inside its mother's womb. An elephant pregnancy lasts nearly two years.

| 1 Womb (uterus) |
| 2 Birth canal |
| 3 Cord links baby to placenta |
| 4 Placenta |

21

Breathing

- **Breathing**, or respiration, is the word used to describe how animals take in oxygen from the air and use it to release energy from the food that they eat.

- **In order to breathe**, gases must pass through part of an animal's body. In mammals, reptiles and birds this happens in the lungs.

- **Fish don't have lungs** – they breathe using gills instead. Oxygen passes through their gills into blood vessels, which carry the oxygen to all parts of the body.

- **An insect's body** is covered in tiny holes. Air enters the holes and oxgyen spreads through the insect in little pipes called trachea. This system of breathing only works well in small animals.

- **Insects that live** in water use gills to breathe.

- **Vertebrates usually have** two lungs, but most snakes have just one fully functioning lung.

- **Marine mammals** hold their breath for a long time when they dive deep into the water, searching for prey.

- **Sperm whales can dive** for more than an hour before they have to come to the surface to breathe.

- **Flying takes a lot** of energy, so birds breathe more slowly than other animals of the same size, but can take in more oxygen with every breath.

- **Frogs and other amphibians** breathe through their moist skin as well as through their lungs.

- **Crabs are able** to use their gills to breathe both in air and underwater.

▼ Gorillas are closely related to humans, so their respiratory system is like ours. Once oxygen has passed into the bloodstream the heart pumps it around the body.

Air moves in and out of the lungs through the nose and the mouth

To make sounds, the vocal cords come together and air moving through the narrow gap makes them vibrate

The ribs play a vital role in protecting the lungs

The diaphragm is like an upturned bowl when relaxed (as shown). As it contracts to inhale, it compresses the stomach and guts below and pushes the belly outwards

23

Excretion

- **When an animal** excretes it is getting rid of the waste food from its body.

- **To gain nutrients** and energy from food, it must be digested, or broken down. This happens in the digestive system.

▼ A bird's waste is called guano. Blue-footed boobies are large seabirds that roost on rocks and cliffs and build their nests from guano. They lay up to three eggs inside a guano nest.

- **Nutrients pass from** the digestive system into the blood, and waste is passed out of the body.

- **When an animal** breathes its body makes a gas called carbon dioxide. Every time an animal breathes out it is removing carbon dioxide from its body.

DID YOU KNOW?

Many animals spray urine to mark their habitats. The distinctive smell tells other animals to stay away!

- **The solid waste** that an animal produces is called faeces.

- **Urine is a waste liquid** that contains water, salt, nitrogen compounds and other substances that the body does not need.

- **Urine is produced** by kidneys, which filter out waste from the blood. Urine is stored in a stretchy organ called the bladder until it is passed from the body.

- **Birds get rid of** extra water and salt through their nostrils.

- **Birds do not** make urine. Instead they produce a soft, solid, white mass that leaves the body through the anus (the opening at the end of the digestive system).

- **Blue whales** eat huge quantities of krill – a pinkish crustacean – and release huge pink plumes of faeces into the ocean.

Life cycles

🐾 **The way that an animal** begins its life, grows, reproduces and dies is called its life cycle.

🐾 **Vertebrates usually live** longer lives than invertebrates, some of which live for just one day as adults.

🐾 **Animals grow** to maturity so that they can reproduce. Once they are adults, most animals don't get any bigger. Snakes, however, keep growing longer as they age.

▶ Young orang-utans stay with their mothers until they are about eight years old. During this 'childhood' a mother teaches her youngster to find food and to build nests in trees for sleeping.

- **An animal's body** is always repairing itself, so new cells are constantly growing to replace old or damaged ones. New blood is made inside bones.

- **When an elephant** dies the rest of its family appears to mourn, as they stand quietly around the dead body. Years later, they sometimes visit the spot where their relative died.

- **Most rodents live** for fewer than three years but naked mole rats have been known to live for 30 years. This makes them the longest-living rodents.

- **It is thought** that bowhead whales may live for up to 200 years.

- **Some male killer whales** and their mothers never separate, and live their entire lives together.

- **Clown anemone fish** begin life as males but some of them change to become females.

- **Similarly**, parrotfish are females when they hatch from their eggs, but some turn into males.

- **An elephant's tusks** keep growing throughout its lifetime.

▶ Parrotfish can change sex, body shape and even colour as they age. It is difficult to tell males and females apart, but mature males often have the most vibrant colours.

Animals in danger

🐾 **When an entire** animal species, or type, dies out completely it is said to be extinct.

🐾 **Animals that are** at risk of becoming extinct are described as endangered, or threatened with extinction.

🐾 **Animals that do not adapt**, or evolve, fast enough to suit a changing environment can become extinct.

🐾 **A mass extinction event** (MEE) occurs when huge numbers of species die out at the same time. This happens when sudden changes on Earth take place, such as a dramatic drop in temperature.

🐾 **There have been** five MEEs so far, but scientists think that the world might be going through another now – caused by humans.

🐾 **Animals struggle** to survive when their habitats are damaged, if they cannot find food or fight disease, and when humans hunt them in large numbers.

▶ *The dodo was a large flightless bird on the island of Mauritius. It probably became extinct in the 1670s because dogs and pigs, which sailors had brought to the island, raided the birds' ground nests and ate the eggs.*

▲ *There are about 8000 adult female hawksbill turtles left in the oceans. Their numbers have fallen by 80 percent in the last 100 years because they have been hunted, their eggs taken for food and their habitats destroyed.*

Pollution may play an important role in the extinction of amphibians. Since 1980 more than 120 species of amphibian have disappeared.

Mountain gorilla numbers fell below 1000 after many years of being hunted by humans. They still face an uncertain future.

Spix's macaw is probably extinct in the wild. None of these birds have been seen since 2000.

The Javan rhinoceros is probably the rarest mammal in the world – there are fewer than 70 left alive in the wild, and none in zoos.

Kakapos are large flightless parrots that have been saved from extinction. There are fewer than 130 birds left and they are guarded from predators on four New Zealand islands.

29

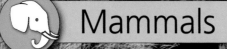

Mammals

What are mammals?

- **Mammals are** a large animal group with furry bodies, bony skeletons and a unique habit of suckling their young on milk.

- **All mammals** are warm-blooded, meaning they can regulate their body temperature so that it stays constant, even in cold weather.

- **Fur and fat** protect mammals from the cold. When they do get cold, they curl up, seek shelter or shiver.

- **Every type of mammal** except monotremes give birth to live young.

▼ American black bears are placental mammals. Females give birth to cubs in January or February and suckle them for 6–8 months.

▼ Etruscan shrews are among the smallest and most active mammals alive today. They grow to just 5 cm long and weigh less than a teaspoon of rice.

🐾 **Most mammals** are placental – their young are nourished inside the mother's womb through an organ called the placenta until they are ready to be born.

🐾 **Marsupials**, a type of mammal, are not placental. Their young are born at an early stage in their development, and are nourished on milk instead of through a placenta.

🐾 **The period of time** from mating to birth is called pregnancy or gestation. In the mammal animal group this varies from 12 days, for some opossums, to 22 months for elephants.

🐾 **About a quarter** of all mammal species are bats.

🐾 **Mammals vary in size** from the finger-sized Etruscan shrew to the blue whale, at 30 m in length.

DID YOU KNOW?
One of the first mammals was a tiny shrew-like creature called Megazostrodon that lived alongside the dinosaurs about 200 million years ago.

Egg-laying mammals

▶ A mature male platypus
is 45–60 cm long. Females
are usually smaller than
males. Their large, broad
tails are used to store fat.

🐾 **Some mammals lay eggs** instead of giving birth to their young. These strange mammals are called monotremes and they all live in, or near, Australia.

🐾 **Duck-billed platypuses** have a broad, flat, beak-like mouth and webbed feet. They live in eastern Australia and Tasmania.

🐾 **After a baby platypus** has hatched from its egg, it sucks on its mother's fur and drinks the milk that oozes out of her skin.

🐾 **Platypuses dig burrows** in riverbanks and are excellent swimmers. Their dense fur is warm and waterproof and they feed on small creatures that they find at the bottom of rivers, streams and lakes.

- **Most monotremes** are nocturnal, which means they are most active between dusk and dawn.

- **Monotremes are one** of only two groups of venomous mammal – the other group is a type of shrew.

- **Male platypuses** have a horned spur on each ankle. Each spur is hollow and filled with venom that causes terrible pain. It is used during self defence, and is powerful enough to kill a dog.

- **There are four species** of echidna, also known as spiny anteaters. Their bodies are covered with spines and their snouts are long and toothless.

- **A female echidna** lays a single egg and puts it in a pouch on her belly. After 10 days, the egg hatches and the baby echidna feeds on its mother's milk.

- **Echidnas feed on small animals** such as worms, ants and termites, but they can survive for weeks without food.

▶ Echidnas have small eyes and rely on a long snout and superb sense of smell to find food. They also use their slender snout rather like a snorkel when they swim across rivers or ponds.

35

Pouched mammals

- **A female marsupial** gives birth to tiny young before taking care of them in a pouch on her body. The young feed on milk while they are in the pouch and continue to grow.

- **Kangaroos**, koalas, American opossums, possums, wombats, bandicoots and bilbies are all marsupials. Lesser-known marsupials include quolls, kowaris, numbats, and potoroos.

- **Many marsupials** live in Australia and the surrounding area. Others live in the Americas.

- **Tasmanian devils** are the largest carnivorous marsupials. They hunt at night and make an eerie screech when disturbed. Their jaws are strong enough to crush bone.

- **There are three species** of wombat. These burrowing animals rely on a diet of grass, so they only give birth when there has been enough rain for grass to grow.

▶ A mother wombat grazes as her baby rests in her pouch. Wombats and other burrowing marsupials have 'upside-down' pouches, so they do not fill up with soil when the animal digs.

▲ *A newborn koala weighs less than 0.5 g. It cannot feed on leaves until it is 5 months old and does not climb out of the pouch until it is 7 months old.*

Virginia opossums give birth to up to 18 young, but they only have enough teats to provide 13 of them with milk. The weakest cannot feed, so they do not survive.

Eastern quolls are slender hunters that have large litters of up 24 young. They once lived in Australia and were common around towns, but are now only found on the island of Tasmania.

Greater gliders leap between eucalyptus trees, and are able to travel distances of more than 100 m.

Kangaroos

🐾 **There are about 70 species** of kangaroos, wallabies and rat kangaroos. They live in Australia, New Guinea and Tasmania.

🐾 **Kangaroos and wallabies** belong to a group of marsupials called macropods – a name that means 'big foot'. They hop around on their large hind limbs.

🐾 **The bones in a kangaroo's legs** prevent it from twisting as it hops, so even if it lands on uneven ground it will not sprain its ankle.

▶ Male kangaroos sometimes battle one another for the right to mate with a female. They stand up and box one another, or use their powerful legs to deliver a mighty kick.

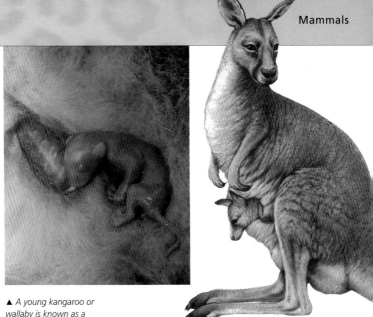

▲ A young kangaroo or wallaby is known as a joey, and it is the size of jellybean at birth. A newborn joey crawls to its mother's pouch, attaches itself to a teat and sucks milk.

▲ A joey stays in its mother's pouch for 4 to 11 months, often climbing out to eat grass or exercise. The mother forces a joey out of the pouch completely when she is ready to give birth again.

🐾 **These animals** are herbivores. They mostly eat grass, leaves, seeds, and fruit. Occasionally, they eat insects and grubs.

🐾 **The red kangaroo** is the largest marsupial, with a body length of up to 1.6 m and a tail length of about one metre.

🐾 **With its extremely** good sense of smell, a red kangaroo is able to detect water even in its dry desert home. A group of kangaroos will travel up to 200 km in their search for water.

Sloths, armadillos and anteaters

🐾 **Sloths and anteaters** have thick, coarse fur and live in Central and South America.

🐾 **Sloths live in trees** and eat plants, but most anteaters live on the ground and eat insects.

🐾 **There are four species** of anteater. They have long, slender snouts and tiny mouths.

🐾 **Anteaters defend themselves** against jaguars and pumas using claws that are up to 10 cm long.

▼ *Giant anteaters can grow to more than 2 m long, including the tail. They have poor eyesight and use their sense of smell to find ants and termites.*

▲ *Sloths are famous slow movers. They hang upside-down from tree branches using long, curved claws. Sloth fur is often tinged with green, as tiny plants called algae live in it.*

When an anteater finds ants and termites to eat, it shoots out its long tongue. The tongue is covered in backward-facing spines and glue-like spit so that the tiny insects stick to it.

Pangolins are similar in size and shape to armadillos. Their bodies are covered with a tough armour of overlapping scales, and they have long tongues for gathering ants and termites.

An anteater's tongue can extend up to 61 cm out of its mouth.

Armadillos belong to an ancient group of mammals and have existed for at least 103 million years.

Giant armadillos have 100 teeth, which is far more than most mammals alive today.

Aardvarks, tenrecs and golden moles

🐾 **Mammals that live** on a diet of insects, such as ants and termites, are called insectivores.

🐾 **There is only one** type of aardvark, and it lives in Africa. Its name means 'earth pig'. These mammals are also known as ant bears.

🐾 **Aardvarks dig for ants**, using their long snouts to sniff for signs of a nest. They have long, sticky tongues for scooping up their prey – they can eat up to 50,000 ants and termites in a single night.

🐾 **Aardvarks have very** long claws for digging. If they are scared they dig a burrow to hide in and can be underground in less than 20 minutes.

◀ An aardvark's body measures about 120 cm long from snout to bottom. These large insectivores are rarely seen in the daytime but they do emerge from their burrows in the winter when it is harder to find food.

◄ Grant's golden moles usually feast on soft-bodied termites, but sometimes hunt larger insects such as locusts. Generally, golden moles feed on whatever small animals they can find.

🐾 **Tenrecs, golden moles** and otter-shrews belong to a group of about 60 species of strange insectivores that are similar to the first mammals that lived.

🐾 **Most tenrecs are** found only on the island of Madagascar. They have poor eyesight but excellent senses of hearing and smell. Some tenrecs have spines.

🐾 **Otter-shrews are tenrecs** that live and hunt in water. They have comb-like toes to groom their fur, keeping it clean and waterproof.

🐾 **Golden moles are small**, blind animals that burrow for insects. Some fully-grown golden moles measure less than 10 cm long.

🐾 **When golden moles** get cold they go into a type of deep rest called torpor, to save energy. They rarely drink water.

▶ Some species of tenrec have spines. If threatened, they roll themselves up like hedgehogs, and hiss at attackers. Streaked tenrecs have spines and patches of dark brown fur.

Otters

- **Otters are small hunting** mammals that are related to weasels. They are one of 58 species of mustelid, the animal group that also includes stoats, skunks and badgers.

- **They live close to water** and are brilliant swimmers, reaching speeds of up to 10 km/h.

- **Otters can close** off their nostrils and ears, allowing them to remain underwater for up to five minutes.

- **They are very lively** creatures, and can often be seen playing on riverbanks and sliding down into the water.

- **Otters can use** their paws to toy with objects such as stones and shellfish.

- **These mammals hunt fish,** usually at night, but they also eat crayfish and crabs, clams and frogs.

- **Otters detect their prey** by sight or touch. They use their long whiskers to detect the vibrations and ripples in the water made by swimming animals.

- **They usually live** in burrows in riverbanks.

- **The giant otter** of Brazil's Amazon river is very rare. It grows up to 1.8 m from its nose to the tip of its tail.

- **Sea otters eat shellfish.** They will balance a rock on their stomach while floating on their back, and crack the shellfish by banging it on the rock.

DID YOU KNOW?
To survive in cold water, a sea otter needs a high-energy diet of at least 100 g of fish an hour.

▼ The hairs in an otter's fur coat are packed together densely to keep out the cold water and trap warm air close to the body. Just one square centimetre contains 70,000 hairs.

Weasels, polecats, minks and skunks

▲ *The least weasel, or European common weasel, is a ferocious hunter. The male is much bigger than the female, which may enable him to eat different prey and avoid competing for the same food.*

The short-tailed weasel (also called the stoat or ermine) turns from brown to white in winter for camouflage against the snow. The tip of its tail stays black.

Although small, weasels and polecats are fierce hunters and able to kill prey much larger than themselves.

Mink feed on a great range of animals, from crabs, fish and small mammals to muskrats, rabbits and birds. Their partly webbed feet enable them to hunt underwater.

🐾 **Martens are agile** and graceful members of the weasel family. Their large paws and sharp claws make them good at climbing trees, while their long, bushy tails help them to balance as they leap from branch to branch.

🐾 **Fishers are a type** of marten that kill porcupines by biting their faces. A kill may take over 30 minutes.

🐾 **The least weasel** is the smallest carnivore, weighing just 50 g. These hunters must eat one third of their bodyweight every day – they can kill and eat rabbits bigger than themselves.

🐾 **Baby weasels** are called kits or kittens.

🐾 **All weasels kill** even if they are not hungry. They store food in underground burrows for times when there is less food available.

🐾 **Weasels and skunks** live throughout the world except Antarctica and Australia.

🐾 **If threatened,** skunks spray a foul-smelling liquid at their predators. The smell lasts for days.

🐾 **Some skunks do handstands** when they spray at attackers, so they can fire their foul liquids a greater distance!

▶ *There are 12 species of skunk and they all have black and white fur. The bold patterns of white stripes and markings warn other animals of their stink.*

Badgers and wolverines

Badgers and wolverines are large members of the mustelid family. There is one species of wolverine and 10 species of badger.

Wolverines have thick fur and live in cold, northerly places around the Arctic. They dig burrows to rest in during the coldest, snowiest nights.

▼ *European badgers live in woodlands. They run along the same routes between their burrows and hunting grounds, creating paths on the woodland floor.*

◀ A wolverine's broad paws spread its weight on the snow, so it can run fast across the landscape as it chases its prey.

🐾 **If a wolverine** has more food than it can eat it stores the meat underground, and returns up to six months later to dig it up again.

🐾 **The wolverine** can kill animals as large as reindeer (caribou). It has highly powerful jaws that can break through thick bones.

🐾 **A European badger** can eat hundreds of earthworms in one night. This species lives in groups of 12 or more in an underground burrow called a sett.

🐾 **Badgers feed on small animals**, as well as fruits, roots, bulbs and also nuts.

🐾 **Badgers that live** in cold countries can survive many winter months without eating. They survive on fat stored in their body during the autumn.

🐾 **Like their close cousins**, the skunks, badgers often have black and white markings.

🐾 **The African ratel**, or honey badger, uses its powerful claws to break open bees' nests to reach the honey inside.

🐾 **The thick**, loose, rubbery skin of the ratel helps to protect it from bee stings and from other predators.

🐾 **Honey badgers** have been known to hunt 3-m-long pythons.

Teeth

🐾 **Most mammals** have teeth that are the optimal size and shape for the type of food they eat. A mammal usually has more than one kind of tooth.

🐾 **Carnivores need sharp**, stabbing canines, or fangs, to plunge into their prey. They also have carnassial teeth, which are large teeth that come together to cut like scissors.

▼ *A warthog's upper tusks look fearsome but the lower teeth actually do more damage in a fight. Bumpy 'warts' on the animal's face help protect it from an attacker's tusks.*

- **Incisors are sharp teeth** at the front of a mammal's mouth. They slice and shear meat, or snip at tough grasses and other plants.

- **Most vertebrates** can grow new teeth throughout their lives.

- **Mammals usually have** just two sets of teeth. The first ones are called milk teeth and they are replaced by adult teeth, which must last the animal its whole life.

- **Teeth are made** of an ultra-tough material called enamel, but they still wear down as the animal ages.

- **Molars and premolars** are the large grinding teeth at the back of a mammal's mouth.

- **An elephant's tusks**, a narwhal's 'horn' and a warthog's tusks are all over-grown teeth. Elephant's tusks are the biggest teeth of any animal living today.

- **Woolly mammoths** – extinct relatives of elephants – had tusks that grew to more than 3 m in length.

- **Most mammals** have 20 to 40 teeth, but giant armadillos have up to 100 teeth and some dolphins have more than 200.

- **Pangolins**, baleen whales and anteaters don't have teeth.

- **Teeth are also** used as weapons for fighting and defence. Sometimes, an animal just needs to show its large, gleaming teeth to scare an attacker away.

Bears

- **There are eight species** of bear. Only two types live south of the Equator – the spectacled bear of South America and the sun bear of Southeast Asia.

- **Although bears** are the largest meat-eating land animals, polar bears are the only ones that only eat meat.

- **Most bears eat a mix** of bugs, meat and plants, while the panda is almost totally herbivorous (plant-eating).

- **There are three types** of brown bear: the Kodiak bear, the grizzly and the Eurasian brown bear. Grizzlies have grey, or 'grizzled' fur on their shoulders.

- **The heaviest bear** is the Kodiak bear, which grows up to 2.8 m in length and weighs up to 725 kg.

▼ *Brown bears fight each other over food, mates or places to live. They prefer to live on their own.*

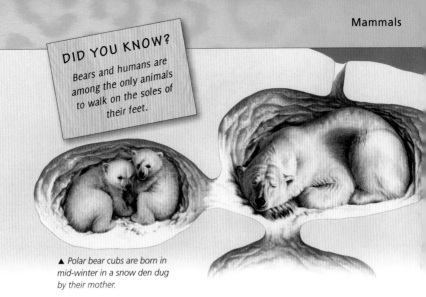

▲ Polar bear cubs are born in mid-winter in a snow den dug by their mother.

🐾 **Brown bears sleep** through the winter when food is scarce. During their winter sleep, bears only breathe around four times per minute, and their heart rate slows to reduce the amount of energy they use.

🐾 **Polar bears** are only the size of guinea pigs when they are born.

🐾 **They feed mainly** on seals, catching them when they come up for air at breathing holes in the Arctic ice. A swipe from a bear's paw and a bite at the back of the skull is enough to kill a seal.

🐾 **Polar bears** are under threat from climate change. The world is warming up and melting the sea ice, which the bears rely on to hunt for seals.

🐾 **The sun bear** of Southeast Asia is the smallest bear, and a very good climber.

Giant pandas

🐾 **Giant pandas** live only in patches of bamboo forest in southwestern China. More than 50 nature reserves protect large areas of their habitat.

🐾 **There are probably** only about 1600 giant pandas in the wild. They are one of the rarest animals in the world.

🐾 **Giant pandas** are threatened by people cutting down their forests. They may also be killed illegally by poachers or caught in traps set for other animals.

🐾 **A giant panda's diet** consists mainly of bamboo. As their digestive systems don't extract the goodness from bamboo well, the bears must eat up to 38 kg of this woody plant per day.

🐾 **Panda cubs** are about the size of hamsters when they are born. They do not open their eyes for 6–8 weeks and are 3 months old before they start to walk.

🐾 **Pandas are good** at swimming and climbing trees. Their strong, curved claws help them to grip tree trunks.

🐾 **A giant panda** has thick, waterproof fur, which keeps it warm in winter. It often snows in winter in the panda's natural home.

🐾 **It was once thought** that giant pandas and red pandas were closely related. Now it is known that giant pandas are bears, and red pandas are the only members of a group within the raccoon family.

▶ *Giant pandas are different to other members of their family. Unlike other bears, pandas do not hibernate in winter and they have thumbs that have developed from wrist bones. They use these thumbs to grip onto bamboo stems.*

DID YOU KNOW?

If a panda loses its grip on a branch and falls, its thick fur helps to cushion its landing.

Wolves

🐾 **The largest of all wild dogs**, wolves hunt in packs to track down animals bigger than themselves, such as moose, caribou (reindeer) and musk oxen.

🐾 **A wolf pack may** have 7–20 wolves, led by a male and female called the alpha pair.

🐾 **A wolf pack's territory** may be 1000 square km or more. Wolves can travel vast distances when hunting.

🐾 **Wolves once lived** throughout Europe and North America. Now they are rare in Europe and are found only in Asia and remote areas of North America.

🐾 **Wolves are the ancestors** of all domestic dogs.

🐾 **Like all dogs**, wolves walk on their toes and have strong claws that do not retract. They are agile and graceful, and can jump distances of up to 4.5 m.

▼ *Only the highest-ranking female wolf in a pack has cubs. She usually has between four and seven cubs, and the whole pack helps to look after them.*

▲ *Grey wolves show a huge range in colour and pale fur is more common in cold, snowy places. Wolves in the U.S. or Russia are often black or dark brown.*

Wolves have very sensitive hearing and can detect sounds up to 3 km away.

Wolves howl to keep in touch with other pack members, before hunting, and to warn rival packs away.

Wolf packs have a distinct hierarchy, reinforced by body language. High-ranking wolves stand tall with ears and tail pointing up. Low-ranking wolves crouch, hold their tail down and flatten their ears against their heads.

In cold areas of North America, Northern Europe and Northern Asia, wolves often have pale coats, which camouflage them against the snow and ice.

Dogs and foxes

🐾 **The dog family** is a large group of four-legged, long-nosed, meat-eating animals. It includes dogs, wolves, foxes, jackals and coyotes.

🐾 **Every kind of dog** has long, pointed canine teeth for piercing and tearing its prey. Canine means 'dog' and 'dog-like'.

▼ *The red fox is a common member of the dog family, found all over Europe, Asia, North America and Australia.*

🐾 **When hunting**, dogs rely mainly on their good sense of smell and acute hearing.

🐾 **African wild dogs** live in packs of 2–30 members. They hunt as a team, which enables them to bring down much larger prey such as antelope or wildebeest.

🐾 **Strong endurance runners**, African wild dogs are able to chase their prey for 5 km or more at speeds of up to 60 km/h. Their sturdy claws grip the ground firmly as they run.

🐾 **The fennec fox** of Africa and the kit fox of North America both have big ears to help them hear their prey at night and keep cool by day.

🐾 **The Arctic fox grows** a white coat in winter, which camouflages it against the winter snow. In summer, when the snow melts, it grows a brown coat instead.

🐾 **Foxes are cunning hunters**. They prowl at night, alone or in pairs. Typical prey includes small mammals such as rats, mice and rabbits.

🐾 **The red fox** has adapted to the growth of towns and cities, and may often be seen at night raiding suburban rubbish bins and dumps.

🐾 **The jackals of Africa** look similar to wolves, but they hunt alone for small prey and only meet in packs to grab the leftovers from the kill of a lion.

Mongooses and meerkats

▲ Mongooses range in size from 24 to 58 cm long. They are agile hunters with lightning reactions that enable them to catch fast-moving prey. Some mongooses even prey on venomous snakes.

🐾 **The mongoose family** includes mongooses, meerkats, and about 77 species of civets, genets and linsangs.

🐾 **Civets and genets** look like cats, with long bodies, short legs and pointed ears. Mongooses and meerkats have long bodies, short legs and rounded ears.

🐾 **The small-spotted genet** hunts rodents, reptiles, insects and birds at night, using its senses of sight, hearing and smell.

- **The Asian binturong** has coarse fur, ear tufts and a grasping (prehensile) tail, which it uses when climbing.

- **Meerkats live in** family groups in burrows or under rocks. They sit up on their back legs to watch for prey or danger.

- **The diet of a meerkat** is wide, and includes insects, arachnids, small mammals, reptiles, birds and plants.

- **The Egyptian mongoose** was sacred to the ancient Egyptians. Paintings of mongooses have been found on tombs and temples that are nearly 5000 years old.

- **Most mongooses** live on their own and usually come out at night. Some species, such as the banded mongoose, live in groups and come out during the daytime.

- **The fossa is rare**, and lives only on the island of Madagascar off the southeast coast of Africa.

- **The fossa hunts lemurs** and other mammals, as well as birds and reptiles.

▶ Meerkat families leave the burrow as the sun rises. They check for danger before setting off to search for food, such as insects, eggs and plants.

61

Hyenas and aardwolves

🐾 **Although hyenas** look like members of the dog family they are more closely related to cats than dogs.

🐾 **Hyenas hunt other** animals to eat but they also scavenge. They live in groups called clans and usually hunt as a pack. This means they can kill animals bigger and stronger than themselves.

🐾 **There are three species** of hyena: the spotted hyena, the brown hyena and the striped hyena. They all live in Africa.

🐾 **Spotted hyena families** are ruled by females and males bow to females when they want to approach them at mating time.

🐾 **Cubs are born black**, with their eyes open. Cubs in the same litter often fight one another – sometimes fatally.

🐾 **A hyena has a small** head but strong, muscular shoulders. Its front legs are longer than its hind legs. The jaws of a hyena are enormous, with large molars and premolars for crushing bone.

◀ *When spotted hyenas hunt as a clan they communicate with one another using whoops and cackles, which is why they are sometimes called 'laughing hyenas'.*

▲ *Aardwolves are smaller than hyenas, rarely measuring more than one metre from snout to tail-tip. They live as families, and males help to look after the cubs by guarding the dens where they sleep.*

It is extremely difficult to tell the difference between male and female hyenas just by looking at them.

Striped hyenas have a woolly mane on their heads and necks. They can raise the hair in the mane to make themselves look bigger in stature.

An aardwolf is a member of the hyena family, but it has bigger ears and weaker jaws than its close cousins.

When an aardwolf is attacked it can defend itself by making a foul-smelling liquid in glands that surround its bottom.

By day, aardwolves hide in rocky crevices or dens left by aardvarks. By night, they hunt for insects, which they gather with their long sticky tongues. They can feast on 300,000 termites in one night.

Lions

- **Lions are one** of the biggest cats, weighing up to 230 kg. A male may be 3 m in length, including his tail.

- **They live mainly in Africa** but about 300–350 Asiatic lions live in the Gir Forest in northwest India.

- **Lions usually live** in grassland or scrub, in family groups called prides. A typical pride contains between three and 10 related females and their cubs, and up to three adult males. The males protect the pride and the females do the hunting.

- **Female lions** are called lionesses. They hunt prey such as gazelle and zebra and even animals as big as buffalo.

🐾 **Lionesses catch their prey** by stealth, stalking to within 30 m of their victims and then dashing forwards to make the kill.

🐾 **A male lion's huge**, shaggy mane makes him look bigger and stronger, and protects him when fighting.

🐾 **The mane of a male** lion begins to grow when he is about two and is fully grown by the time he is five.

🐾 **Male lion cubs** leave the pride when they are two years old, and have to fight an older male to join another pride.

🐾 **Lions usually rest** for about 20 hours a day, and walk no farther than 10 km or so a day.

🐾 **They often hunt** at dusk or dawn, and have very good night vision.

▼ Like all cats, lions are supreme predators. Their forward-facing eyes help them to spy and focus on prey far away, even when the light is fading.

DID YOU KNOW?
A male lion is able to drag a 300 kg zebra along the ground – it would take at least six men to do this.

65

Tigers

🐾 **Tigers are the largest** of the big cats, with huge heads. The average male tiger's body grows to over 2 m in length, plus a one-metre-long tail.

▼ *The Amur, or Siberian, tiger is the largest of all tigers. At one time, the number of Amur tigers fell to 40 after they had been hunted for their beautiful fur. Today they are mostly protected from poachers and there are about 450 in the wild.*

- **They live in Asia**, but are becoming rare as their forest homes are destroyed and poachers kill them illegally. There are approximately 4000 adult tigers left in the wild.

- **Tigers prey on large animals** such as deer, buffalo, antelope and wild pigs. They hunt silently at night, stalking their prey, then making a sudden bound.

- **Although they are fast** and strong, they tire quickly, and give up if they fail to catch their prey first time.

- **Adult tigers** usually live alone. Males try to keep other males out of their territory, but when two tigers meet, they may rub one another's head in greeting.

- **A male tiger's territory** often includes that of two or three females, but they only meet to mate.

- **Tigers mark out their** territory by scratching trees and urinating on them.

- **Between two and four cubs** are usually born at a time. The cubs are playful, and totally dependent on their mother for 2–3 years.

- **A tiger's stripes** provide good camouflage in long grass and under trees. Each tiger has its own unique pattern of stripes.

- **Tigers are good swimmers** and often lie in rivers to cool off on hot days.

Leopards

🐾 **Leopards live in Africa**, the Middle East and central and southern Asia. They survive in a variety of habitats, from grassland and forests to deserts and mountains.

🐾 **Most leopards** have rosette-shaped spots. The black leopard, or 'black panther', has a dark coat so the spots are hard to see.

🐾 **They live on their own** and usually hunt at night. Leopards lie in wait for their prey or stalk until they are close enough to make the final attack.

🐾 **Leopards hunt** a great range of prey, such as monkeys, snakes, birds, fish and chickens.

🐾 **They are good climbers** and will drag large prey into trees to prevent other animals from stealing it.

▶ *A snow leopard's tail is nearly one metre long. Its under-fur is 12 cm thick so it can survive in temperatures of -40° C.*

DID YOU KNOW?

Cats find it much easier to climb up a tree than down it because of the shape of their curved claws.

Female leopards usually give birth to two or three cubs. The cubs stay with their mother until they are at least 18 months old.

If a mother leopard senses danger, she picks each of her cubs up by the scruff of their necks and carries them in her mouth to a place of safety.

Snow leopards are more closely related to tigers than leopards but do not roar like other big cats.

The snow leopard lives in the Himalayan Mountains. It has large paws to help it walk on the snow and its long tail is useful for balance on steep, slippery slopes.

There are only between 3500 and 7000 snow leopards left. They are threatened by people farming and hunting in the mountains. Snow leopards are still hunted for their thick fur and for their bones, which are used in some traditional 'medicines'.

▶ Leopards have a head-body length of 1–2 m. They are superb climbers and often sleep in trees.

Jaguars and pumas

- **The jaguar** is the largest South American cat and grows up to 2.6 m in length, including the tail.

- **It has a heavier** build than the leopard, with a broader head, strong legs and powerful paws. It has black marks inside each rosette, unlike the leopard.

- **Jaguars swim** and climb well, often lying in wait for prey on tree branches. They also stalk prey on the ground, waiting until they are close before pouncing.

- **They catch animals** such as peccaries, deer, monkeys, tapirs, birds, turtles, caiman, frogs and fish.

- **Female jaguars give birth** to a litter of up to four young in a den among rocks or in a hole.

- **Young jaguars** stay with their mother for about two years while they learn how to survive on their own.

- **Although jaguars can roar**, they are more likely to grunt, growl, snarl or even mew.

◀ *The dark circles on a cat's fur are called rosettes but a jaguar's patterned fur also has stripes, blotches and spots. These complex patterns and colours help to camouflage the cat in the dappled shadows of its jungle home.*

- **The puma**, or mountain lion, of the Americas lives in a variety of habitats from mountains and forests to swamps and grasslands.

- **It is the biggest** North American cat, with a tail up to 78 cm long.

- **The puma has sandy** or grey-brown fur, without any spots or stripes, although the kittens are spotted when they are born, for camouflage.

- **Pumas are also known** as cougars. They hiss, growl, purr and scream but they cannot roar.

- **If a puma cannot** finish its meal it drags the remains of the carcass (dead body) to a safe hiding place and buries it under leaves to eat later.

▼ *Pumas live as far north as Alaska and as far south as Chile and Argentina. They are most active between dusk and dawn, and can travel 10 km in one night, searching for food.*

Cheetahs

- **The fastest land animal**, the cheetah can reach 100 km/h in just four seconds.

- **Cheetahs have flexible bodies**, stong shoulders and long legs. Their tails helps with balance when sprinting.

- **Their claws do not retract**. They act like spikes on running shoes, helping the cheetah grip the ground.

- **They quickly overheat** so cheetahs have to halt their chases after about a minute. Chases usually last 20 seconds.

- **Cheetahs hunt during** the day and sight is their most important sense for hunting.

- **They feed mainly** on grazing mammals, knocking them to the ground and suffocating them with a throat bite.

▶ Cheetahs are built for speed. As a cheetah runs its spine bends, bringing the hind legs far forwards for longer strides. Cheetahs can twist and turn to change direction in a second, while keeping their eyes fixed on the prey.

- **Cheetahs often drag** their prey to a hiding place before eating to stop vultures stealing it.

- **Female cheetahs** give birth to an average of three cubs, which weigh about 300 g and are up to 30 cm in length.

- **A mother cheetah** carries her cubs in her mouth to a new hiding place every few days. This helps to keep them safe from predators.

- **Adult female cheetahs** live on their own, or with their cubs. Males live in groups, sometimes with their brothers.

DID YOU KNOW?

About 12,000 years ago nearly all the cheetahs died out. Today's cheetahs are descended from the handful that survived.

Small cats

🐾 **Small cats crouch down** when they feed, whereas big cats lie down to feed. At rest, small cats bend their paws under their bodies and wrap their tails around themselves. Big cats place their paws in front of their bodies when they rest and stretch their tails out behind them.

▼ *The Scottish wildcat is a type of European wildcat. Long ago, Scottish wildcats were worshipped as forest spirits and even today it is said they cannot be tamed. Fewer than 100 survive in the wild.*

🐾 **The lynx lives in** cold northern lands. It has thick fur to keep it warm, wide feet to stop it sinking into the snow and long legs to help it travel through deep snow.

🐾 **The European wildcat** looks similar to a striped pet cat, but has a bushy tail with a rounded tip and a larger head, with bigger eyes.

🐾 **Most cats don't like water** but the fishing cat spends most of its life in and around rivers and streams. It has partly webbed front paws and feeds on fish.

🐾 **The caracal is very good** at catching birds, jumping up to knock low-flying birds right out of the air.

🐾 **Male ocelots stay** with the females after mating and help to look after the kittens by bringing food to the den.

🐾 **The serval of Africa** uses its sensitive hearing to listen for the rustling sounds made by its prey, before making the final pounce.

🐾 **Sand cats stay in burrows** during the heat of the day, emerging at night to hunt insects, lizards, birds and mice. Their furry feet give them a good grip on the sand.

🐾 **Bobcats live in North America** and Mexico. They have very short tails and tufts on their ears. There are up to one million bobcats living in the United States.

🐾 **Marbled cats are similar** to clouded leopards. They live in Southeast Asia but they are very shy and little is known about how they live.

Moles, shrews and hedgehogs

- **Hedgehogs and shrews** are called insectivores because, like some other mammals, they survive by mostly eating a diet of insects. Moles also eat worms and slugs.

- **Most insectivores** are solitary and come out at night. They have long snouts and a good sense of smell.

- **Hedgehogs are protected** by a coat of spiny quills, which are actually modified hairs. They roll up into a ball to hide their soft underparts.

▼ *A strange-looking star-nosed mole has 22 fleshy 'tentacles' growing from its snout. As the mole burrows the tentacles move rapidly, and the mole uses them like fingers to feel for prey.*

◄ Hedgehogs can attack and eat adder snakes, as they are immune to their venom. Usually, however, they hunt smaller prey. Their prickles defend them against predators.

🐾 **Baby hedgehogs are born** with about 150 spines beneath the skin so they don't harm their mother during the birth process. By the time they are three days old, the spines have broken through the skin.

🐾 **Hedgehogs that live** in colder places go into a deep sleep (hibernation) over winter. This helps them survive the cold months, when their insect food is not available.

🐾 **Water shrews dive** underwater to catch fish, small frogs and small water creatures.

🐾 **Some shrews have** a poisonous bite. The American short-tailed shrew produces enough poison to kill 200 mice.

🐾 **Moles spend most** of their lives underground, relying on keen senses of touch and smell to find worms and beetles.

🐾 **The molehills on the surface** are heaps of soil that moles have dug out of their tunnels. The nest is underneath a large, more permanent molehill called a fortress.

🐾 **Desmans are swimming moles**. They have waterproof fur, webbed toes and a flattened tail fringed with stiff hairs. They can close their nose and ears underwater.

Rabbits, hares and pikas

🐾 **Rabbits, hares and pikas** all belong to a group of mammals called lagomorphs, which means 'hare-shaped'.

🐾 **Lagomorphs have long**, soft fur and furry feet. They have large ears and their eyes are high on the sides of their head, giving them a wide field of vision.

▶ *Hares that live in northerly places, such as snowshoe, Arctic, mountain and Japanese hares often grow white fur in winter.*

- **Hares live above ground** and escape enemies through sheer speed. Rabbits live in burrows underground.

- **Baby hares are born** above ground, covered in fur and with their eyes open. Rabbits are born hairless and blind in burrows.

- **Rabbits and hares** have very long back legs to help them run away from danger. Some large hares can reach speeds of 80 km/h.

- **If a rabbit senses danger**, it thumps the ground loudly with its back feet to warn other rabbits.

- **The front teeth** (incisors) of lagomorphs grow continuously throughout their lives but are worn down by gnawing tough plant food.

- **The black-tailed jackrabbit** lives in the desert. Its huge, thin ears act like radiators to get rid of body heat and cool the animal down.

- **Pikas are lively**, agile mammals that are active during the day. They live high in the mountains or below the ground in deserts.

- **During the summer and autumn**, pikas build haystacks of plant material to last them through the winter. They do not hibernate.

Small rodents

◀ *The field vole is a herbivore, feeding on berries, seeds, leaves, roots, and stems. It has a characteristically short tail.*

🐾 **Rodents are the largest** group of mammals – there are about 2000 species. The group includes voles, lemmings, squirrels, beavers, rats and porcupines.

🐾 **All rodents have two pairs** of razor-sharp front teeth for gnawing nuts and berries, and a set of ridged teeth in their cheeks for chewing.

🐾 **A rodent's front teeth** (incisors) grow continuously, but gnawing keeps them the same length. Rodents get their name from the Latin word for gnawing, *rodere*.

🐾 **Rats and mice** are by far the most common rodents – they have adapted well to living alongside humans.

🐾 **A mouse can produce** up to 34 young in one litter.

🐾 **North American prairie dogs** live in a network of underground burrows called a 'town'. Thousands can live in a single town.

🐾 **Kangaroo rats from** the North American deserts hardly ever drink. They get most of their water from their food and also save water by coming out at night when the air is cool and moist.

🐾 **The woodland jumping** mouse is less than 10 cm long, but it can jump up to 3 m at a time. Jumping mice have been known to hibernate for nine months in one year.

🐾 **African dormice** can lose their tails if they are attacked. A predator is left holding onto the fluffy tail while the dormouse escapes.

▼ *Alpine marmots live in mountains with very cold winters.*
They hibernate in burrows for up to nine months of the year.

Large rodents

- **Beavers are large rodents** with flat, paddle-like tails. They live in northern America and northern Eurasia.

- **Incredibly strong front** teeth allow beavers to chop down quite large trees. They gnaw around the tree in a ring until it finally crashes down.

- **Beavers build dams** across streams using tree branches laid onto a base of mud and stones. Families of beavers often work together on a dam.

- **Porcupines have hard hairs** called quills on their backs. These can be up to 35 cm in length and have sharp tips. If the quills stick into an attacker's skin, they cause serious wounds.

- **The world's largest rodent** is the capybara. It weighs up to 75 kg but is a good swimmer in the rivers of Central and South America.

- **North American porcupines** climb trees so they can feed on bark and the needles (leaves) of conifers.

- **The mara is a large rodent** that looks like a cross between a hare and an antelope. Maras live in South America and they mate for life, which is unusual in the rodent family.

▶ Beavers play an important role in developing watery habitats for other animals. They slow a river's flow, help to keep the water clean and create wetland areas where birds and amphibians can thrive.

🐾 **The fur of a chinchilla** is thick and velvety soft. Up to 60 hairs can grow from a single follicle (the part of the skin where one hair would normally grow).

🐾 **Chinchillas have been** hunted for their fur, which means they are in danger of becoming extinct in the wild.

Bats

- **Bats are the only flying** mammals. Their wings are made of leathery skin stretched between four long finger bones on each hand. Fast-flying bats can reach speeds of almost 100 km/h.

- **Most bats sleep** during the day, hanging upside down in caves and other dark places. They emerge at night to hunt for insects.

- **Bats find things** in the dark by giving out a series of high-pitched clicks. They can locate prey from the echoes (sounds that bounce back to them) of the clicks. This is called echolocation.

- **Most bats rely** on their excellent eyesight to avoid predators and some need vision to find food.

- **There are more than** 1100 species of bat, living on all continents except Antarctica. One species in every four mammals is a bat!

- **Kitti's hog-nosed bat** is probably the world's smallest mammal. Its body is only about 2.5 cm in length and it is so small it could sit on the tip of your finger.

- **Many tropical flowers** rely on fruit bats to spread their pollen.

- **Frog-eating bats** can tell edible frogs from poisonous ones by the frogs' mating calls.

- **False vampire bats** are bats that do not suck on blood, but feed on other creatures such as smaller bats and rats. The greater false vampire bat of Southeast Asia is one of the biggest of all bats.

DID YOU KNOW?

Most mammals' knees bend the same way as ours, but a bat's knees bend backwards.

▲ The huge ears of this big-eared bat catch the sounds reflected from its surroundings.

Vampire bats

🐾 **Vampire bats live in** Central and South America. There are three species: hairy-legged and white-winged vampire bats feed on bird blood, but common vampire bats feed on mammal blood.

🐾 **Like other bats**, vampire bats live in groups called colonies and usually roost in dark places such as caves, buildings and hollow trees.

▼ *A vampire bat has a flattened snout. This allows it to get its teeth and mouth really close to its victim's flesh as it laps up blood. The bat's bite is not painful so a victim does not notice that it has been attacked.*

- **A female vampire** bat gives birth to just one pup at a time and she feeds it with her milk until it is about six months old.

- **Cattle and horses** are a vampire bat's usual prey. They find their victims by sensing their body heat and by listening for the sound of their breathing.

DID YOU KNOW?
Vampire bats have amazing hearing. Some can hear the sound of an insect walking on a leaf.

- **It is rare for vampire bats** to attack humans. Their bites are dangerous because vampire bats spread diseases, especially rabies.

- **Vampire bats** have special places on their noses that can sense the heat given off by another animal.

- **Once they have found** a victim, they use their razor-sharp incisor teeth to slice off a slither of skin. As the blood flows out, the vampire bat laps it up.

- **As a vampire bat** feeds its saliva enters the wound and keeps the blood flowing freely.

- **Once a bat has fed** it returns to its colony and regurgitates (vomits) some of its blood meal to share with members of its family.

- **A vampire bat can starve** to death in just three days if it has not been able to get a meal, or persuade one of its colony to share their blood meal.

Lemurs and lorises

- **Lemurs and lorises** belong to a group of mammals called primates, along with monkeys, apes and humans. They have smaller brains and a better sense of smell than their primate relatives.

- **Lemurs live only** on the islands of Madagascar and Comoros, off the African east coast.

- **Most lemurs are active at night** and live in trees, but the ring-tailed lemur lives on the ground and is active by day.

▼ A ring-tailed lemur mother usually has just one baby at time. It feeds on its mother's milk until it is about four months old.

◀ Slow lorises have flat faces, round heads, small ears and thick fur. They grip onto branches with their hands as they clamber slowly through the forests of Asia. Slow lorises eat plants, spiders and insects.

🐾 **Most lemurs eat fruit**, leaves and insects but some eat only bamboo or nectar.

🐾 **The largest primate** on Madagascar is the indri. This large lemur also has a very loud song that can be heard more than 2 km away. Indris sing to tell other indris to keep out of their area of forest.

🐾 **In the mating season**, ring-tailed lemurs have stink fights for females, rubbing their wrists and tails in stink glands under their arms and rear – then waving them at rivals to drive them off.

🐾 **Lorises and pottos** are furry, big-eyed primates of the forests of Asia and Africa. All are brilliant climbers.

🐾 **Bushbabies are the acrobats** of the loris family. They get their name because their cries sound like a human baby crying.

🐾 **Bushbabies are nocturnal** animals and their big eyes help them see in the dark.

🐾 **Tarsiers of Southeast Asia** are small, huge-eyed primates. They have very long fingers and can turn their heads halfway round to look backwards.

Old World monkeys

Monkeys are primates – mammals that are mainly adapted for living in the trees. They have long arms and legs and flexible fingers for gripping branches.

Most monkeys have tails, unlike apes.

Monkeys from Africa and Asia are called Old World monkeys. They include baboons, langurs and macaques.

Old World monkeys have close-set nostrils and hard pads on their bottoms to help them sleep comfortably sitting up.

The tail of an Old World monkey does not grasp branches, like that of a New World monkey (a monkey from the rainforests of Central and South America).

Japanese macaques live in the mountains, where it gets very cold. They grow thick coats, and sit in the hot water bubbling up from volcanic springs to keep warm.

The proboscis monkey gets it name from the huge nose of the male (proboscis is another word for nose), which probably helps it to attract females.

Baboons are large African monkeys. They spend most of their time on the ground. They are strong and agile enough to catch other monkeys, birds and small antelopes.

Colobus monkeys have long back legs that help them to leap great distances between trees. The tail of the black and white colobus helps it to steer and change direction.

Male mandrills have bright red and blue faces, and females prefer males with brighter colours. Mandrills are the heaviest monkeys in the world, weighing up to 55 kg.

▼ A male mandrill opens its mouth wide, bares its teeth and spreads its arms when it wants to frighten another animal away. A big yawn can also be a sign of friendliness between mandrills.

New World monkeys

🐾 **Monkeys from the rainforests** of Central and South America are called New World monkeys.

🐾 **New World monkeys** include howler monkeys, spider monkeys, woolly monkeys and capuchins, as well as marmosets and tamarins.

▼ *Squirrel monkeys spend almost all their lives in trees and rarely come to the ground. They are so light and nimble they can run along branches that are no more than 2 cm thick.*

- **New World monkeys have wide**, round nostrils that are set far apart, and no sitting pads.

- **They often have muscular tails** that can grip like hands. These tails are described as 'prehensile'.

- **A spider monkey** can hang from branches by its tail, which has a bare patch of skin near the tip, to help it grip.

- **Unlike most monkeys**, the douroucouli (owl monkey) is nocturnal. It has big eyes to help it see in the dark.

- **Capuchin monkeys** are very intelligent. They even use tools such as rocks to crack open nuts and shells.

- **Squirrel monkeys** are highly active, leaping through the trees like squirrels. They live in large groups of up to 200 individuals.

- **Saki monkeys** have long fur to protect them from heavy rain in the forests. The monk saki has long fur around its face, making it look like it is wearing a hood, like a monk.

- **Marmosets and tamarins** live only in Central and South America. They are primates, but they do not have grasping hands and feet. They run along the tops of branches instead of clinging and have claws at the end of their long fingers.

Intelligence

- **Intelligence is an important** characteristic of all primates. Although it is difficult to measure intelligence, primates have large brains, are able to learn new things and solve problems.

- **Clever animals have complex** methods of communicating – 'talking' to each other. A monkey may hoot, for example, to tell its family that a predator is nearby.

- **A brain uses up** to one quarter of an animal's energy, so an animal with a big brain needs extra food to fuel its brain power.

- **One part of intelligence** is memory. Clever animals may remember a good place to find water, even if they have not visited the place in many years.

▶ Chimpanzees poke grass stems and sticks into rotting wood or mounds of earth and pick out termites that live there. They also use rocks to smash hard fruits or nuts.

- **Clever animals** can learn new things. Elephants learn how to use tree trunks to destroy electric fences so they can walk into farmers' fields and eat crops.

- **Primates such as orang-utans**, chimps and bonobos have been taught to communicate with humans using sign language.

- **Grey parrots** can copy human language, mimic human speech and can even understand simple words and phrases.

- **Some animals**, including dolphins and primates, are able to use tools. Capuchin monkeys, for example, use rocks to smash nuts open.

Lesser apes

🐾 **Gibbons are known as lesser apes** because they are smaller and lighter than the great apes, such as gorillas and chimpanzees.

🐾 **Like the great apes**, gibbons do not have a tail.

🐾 **Gibbons live high up in the trees** and hardly ever come down to the ground. They use their long arms to swing quietly from branch to branch at speeds of up to 56 km/h. This way of moving is called 'brachiation'.

🐾 **Special wrist bones** allow gibbons to turn their bodies as they swing through the trees while keeping a tight grip on the branches.

🐾 **There are 14 different species of gibbon**, which all live in the forests of Asia.

🐾 **Siamangs are the biggest gibbons**, weighing up to 14 kg. They sing to tell other gibbons where they live. Their throat pouches swell with air as they sing, making their calls very loud.

🐾 **They feed mainly on fruit**, but gibbons also eat leaves, shoots, buds, flowers and occasionally insects and eggs.

◄ Gibbons spend their lives in trees and have long arms and strong shoulders to support their weight as they swing.

🐾 **Gibbons are the only apes** to live in pairs and stay with the same partner for life. The young do not leave their parents until they are six or seven years old.

🐾 **They are the only apes** that do not build nests. Instead, gibbons sleep sitting up on the branches, resting on their tough sitting pads.

🐾 **Male and female hoolock gibbons** have different-coloured fur. Adult males are blackish-brown, while adult females are yellowish-brown. Newborn hoolock gibbons are a greyish-white colour.

Great apes

🐾 **Apes are our closest relatives** in the animal world. The great apes are gorillas, chimpanzees, orang-utans and bonobos. Humans are sometimes called the fifth great ape.

🐾 **Like humans, great apes have long arms,** and fingers and toes for gripping. They are clever and can use sticks and stones as tools.

🐾 **Gorillas are the biggest** of all the great apes, weighing up to 225 kg and standing as tall as 2 m. But they are gentle herbivores and eat leaves and shoots.

🐾 **Mountain gorillas live in Central Africa** in Uganda and on the borders of Uganda, Rwanda and the Democratic Republic of Congo. There are only about 700 of them left.

🐾 **When danger threatens a gorilla troop,** the leading adult male stands upright, pounds his hands against his chest, and bellows loudly.

◄ *Male gorillas are up to twice the size of females. Dominant males defend and control family groups of females and their young.*

🐾 **Between 20,000 and 30,000** orang-utans remain in the forests of Borneo and Sumatra.

🐾 **These highly intelligent** great apes could be extinct in as little as five or ten years if their habitat continues to be destroyed at the same rate.

🐾 **Bonobos look similar** to chimpanzees but are slimmer, with longer legs, smaller heads and black faces.

🐾 **In contrast to the male-dominated** chimpanzee groups, bonobo groups are led by females and are much more peaceful. Bonobos also spend more time in the trees than chimpanzees.

▶ Grooming each other's fur helps bonobos to relax and strengthens friendships.

Chimpanzees

Chimpanzees live in the forests of western and central Africa. They are noisier and fight more often than the other great apes.

They are very clever and use tools more than any other animal, apart from humans. Chimpanzees use leaves as sponges to soak up water to drink, and they crack nuts with stones.

Chimpanzees communicate with each other by means of a huge range of different grunts and screams. They also communicate through facial expressions and hand gestures, just as humans do. Experiments have shown chimpanzees can learn to respond to many words.

Adult male chimpanzees are strong and can be violent. They sometimes fight each other, and battle with chimps from other families.

Male chimps can fight to the death and even kill baby chimps and females.

Chimps spend half of their time looking for food and eating. They mostly eat leaves, fruits, seeds and berries but they also eat insects and other small animals.

Sometimes males hunt as a pack to find and kill monkeys to eat.

Female chimpanzees have their first baby when they are about 13 years old.

🐾 **At night**, chimpanzees build nests in a tree by breaking and bending branches to create a soft 'bed'.

🐾 **Chimps often get bald heads** as they get older, but females lose more hair than males.

▼ Chimps use their faces to show how they are feeling. An open mouth, with the lips over the teeth, shows that a chimp is playing. Young chimps love to wrestle, stroke and tickle each other. These activities help them to form close bonds as adults.

Horses and ponies

- **Horses are four-legged**, hooved animals, now bred mainly for human use.

- **Adult male horses** are called stallions, females are called mares and babies are called foals.

- **Przewalski's horse** looks similar to the wild horses that roamed the grasslands of Europe and northern Asia until a few thousand years ago. Today, they survive mainly in zoos.

▼ Semi-wild white horses roam the marshlands of the Camargue, in southern France. Camargue horses are hardy, and are able to survive on a tough diet of marsh reeds.

- **The mustangs** (wild horses) of the United States are descended from tame horses.

- **Tame horses are of three main kinds** – light horses for riding (such as Morgans and Arabs), heavy horses for pulling ploughs and wagons (such as Percherons and Shire horses), and ponies (such as Shetlands).

- **Ponies are small horses**, between 10 and 15 hands high (a hand is 10 cm). They are often used to teach children how to ride.

- **Lipizzaners are beautiful white horses**. Many are trained to jump and dance at the Spanish Riding School in Vienna.

- **The Shire horse is the largest horse**, growing up to 2 m in height and weighing over one tonne.

- **A horse has all its permanent teeth** by the age of five or six. This includes 12 molars (grinding teeth) and six incisors (cutting teeth). A horse can be aged accurately by its teeth up to the age of ten years old.

- **Quarter horses are agile horses** used by cowhands for cutting out (sorting cows from the herd). They got their name from running quarter-mile races.

Wild equids

- **Horses, ponies, zebras** and asses all belong to the same animal family – the equids.

- **The African wild ass** is the ancestor of the domestic donkey. Donkeys are very strong for their size and are used in some countries for carrying heavy loads.

- **Like horses,** zebras and asses have a single toe on each foot. The horse family's nearest relatives are rhinos and tapirs, which also take their weight on a long, central toe.

- **Zebras are noisy,** inquisitive African mammals. They live in family groups of between two and 20 members. People have never managed to tame zebras.

- **There are three species of zebra** – common, mountain and Grevy's. Each has a different pattern of stripes.

- **Zebras bite or kick** rival zebras during the mating season. They also kick out at predators, such as lions.

- **Wild asses live on the deserts** and scrublands of central Asia, the Middle East and North Africa. They can go for long periods without drinking.

- **The largest wild ass**, the kiang, develops a layer of fat for winter. This keeps it warm and provides a food store.

- **The female African wild ass** gives birth to a single foal. She lives in a troop with other females and their young.

- **Mules are the offspring** of a male donkey and a female horse. They are strong and are used for carrying heavy loads.

▼ *Common zebras are also known as plains zebras. They travel as herds, searching for grass and water.*

Rhinoceroses

- **Rhinoceroses are big**, tough-skinned animals of Africa and southern Asia. They are the world's largest land animals after elephants.

- **Rhinos are herbivores**: they eat plants, especially grass, leaves and twigs.

- **The African black rhino** can weigh up to 1.5 tonnes.

- **African black and white rhinos** and the smaller Sumatran rhino have two horns in the middle of their heads. Indian and Javan rhinos have just one.

- **A rhino's horn** is mostly made up of keratin, the same substance that is in hair, nails and horses' hooves. It also contains calcium, one of the minerals that make teeth hard.

- **Sumatran rhinos** are the smallest of all rhinos and their thick skin is covered with a coat of coarse brown hair.

- **Indian rhinos** came close to extinction in the early 20th century, and their population dropped to fewer than 200 individuals. After conservation efforts their numbers have now increased to about 3000.

- **Rhinos rely** on their senses of smell and hearing. They have poor eyesight and cannot see a person more than 30 m away.

DID YOU KNOW?
The African white rhinoceros' front horn can grow to an incredible 1.5 m in length.

🐾 **Javan and Sumatran rhinos** are almost extinct and the other three rhinos are increasingly threatened by habitat destruction and the demand for their horns.

▼ *Numbers of black rhinos have decreased dramatically from about 65,000 in 1970 to only about 4880 today. Some gamekeepers have cut off the rhinos' horns to make them less of a target for poachers.*

Hippopotamuses

🐾 **Hippopotamuses are big**, grey, pig-like creatures that live in Africa. They have the biggest mouth of any land animal.

🐾 **When a hippo yawns** its mouth gapes wide enough to swallow a sheep whole, but they only eat grass.

🐾 **Hippos spend their days** wallowing in rivers and swamps, and only come out at night to feed.

🐾 **A hippo's eyes**, ears and nose are all on the top of its head, and so remain above the water when the rest of its body is completely submerged.

🐾 **The word hippopotamus** comes from the ancient Greek words for horse, *hippo*, and river, *potamos*.

🐾 **Hippos have unusual skin** that loses water very easily. If a hippo didn't spend most of its time in water its skin would quickly dry out and start to crack.

🐾 **Their skin makes** its own 'suncream' which turns red in the air.

🐾 **There are two species of hippo**. Common hippos are about 3 m long and live on grasslands. Pygmy hippos are up to 1.75 m long and live in the forests of western Africa.

🐾 **Although hippos have wide**, barrel-shaped bodies like pigs they are more closely related to whales.

🐾 **Hippos can be aggressive**, and readily attack animals, including humans, that come too close.

🐾 **Sometimes males fight** one another to the death, using lower canines that measure up to 50 cm.

◀ *Ticks are little bugs that burrow into an animal's skin and suck blood. Red-billed oxpecker birds remove the ticks and feed on the blood that oozes out of the hippopotamus's skin.*

Pigs

🐾 **Members of the pig family** are mostly short-legged, strong and clever animals. They eat a wide range of foods and live in forests or woods.

🐾 **The pig family includes** wild boars, hogs and warthogs as well as the extraordinary babirusa. This wild pig has long, curling tusks that grow out through the top of its snout.

🐾 **Wild pigs and boars** have four toes on each foot. Their long snouts bear a set of tusks and end in a disc with two large nostrils.

🐾 **Wild boars** were first kept as farm animals 11,000 years ago. Modern farm pigs are descended from wild boars that were bred for meat.

▼ *Wild boars grow warm, thick coats in the winter. They originally came from Europe and Asia but are now found on every continent except Antarctica.*

▶ The bearded pig sometimes goes on migrations. In 1983–1984, a group of one million bearded pigs travelled about 200 km.

- **Pigs are clever animals** with very long memories. They are one of the few animals that seem to recognize reflections in a mirror.

- **Warthogs mostly eat grass**, and they even use their snouts like shovels to dig into the soil to reach the roots of grass plants.

- **Peccaries are long-legged** pig-like animals that live in tropical forests of the Americas in herds of up to 400.

- **Peccaries eat plants**, and some types survive on a diet of cacti, despite their prickly spines.

- **A female pig** is called a sow, a male is a boar and the young are called piglets. A herd of sows and their young is called a sounder.

Cattle, goats and sheep

- **Cattle, goats and sheep** belong to the bovid family. There are nearly 300 species of bovid and they are found throughout the world, although they are most common in Africa. Antelopes are also bovids.

- **If a lion attacks** an African buffalo calf the rest of the herd gather together to mob the predator and defend the youngster.

- **Adult buffaloes** have huge curved horns.

- **Thanks to its thick,** heavy coat of fur a yak can survive the harsh environment of cold, wind-swept grasslands in Tibet and China.

- **An American bison** measures 2 m tall from its hooves to the top of its massive shoulders.

- **There were once** 50 million bison living on the American grasslands, but hunting brought them close to extinction.

- **Male musk oxen** produce a strong smell when it is mating time. They have large horns and battle each other over the right to mate with a female.

- **The largest horns** on any living animal belong to the Indian water buffalo. One animal was found to have horns measuring 4.24 m from one tip to the other.

- **Mountain goats** are fast and agile creatures, even on slippery cliff edges. Their large hooves have soft pads in the centre and hard rims for grip.

🐾 **The fur of a Barbary sheep** is reddish-brown. It grows a long beard on its chin and throat, which can reach down to the sheep's hooves.

🐾 **The horns of a male** Alpine ibex grow to 1.4 m long.

🐾 **The two long**, curly horns of a bighorn sheep can weigh as much as the rest of the animal's skeleton.

▶ The ibex belongs to a group of animals called goat antelopes. Males are bigger and heavier than females and spend the day on high mountain slopes, in groups of six to eight. Females live further down the mountain, in herds of up to 20.

Camels

- **Camels are the biggest** desert mammals and they have adapted to live in extremely dry conditions.

- **Dromedary camels** have one hump and live mainly in the Sahara Desert and the Middle East. Bactrian camels live in central Asia and have two humps.

DID YOU KNOW?
Camels are said to have by far the worst-smelling breath in the entire animal kingdom.

🐾 **A camel's hump** is made of fat, but its body can break the fat down into food and water when these are scarce.

🐾 **Camels can go for many days** or even months without water. But when water is available, they can drink over 200 l in a day.

🐾 **Camels sweat very little**, to save liquid. Instead, their body temperature rises by as much as 6°C when it is hot.

🐾 **Their feet have** two joined toes to stop them sinking into soft sand or soft snow.

🐾 **A camel's nostrils** can close up completely to block out sand.

🐾 **They have a double row** of eyelashes to protect their eyes from sand and sunlight.

🐾 **A camel's stomach is huge**, with three different sections. Like cows, camels are ruminants – they partially digest food, then bring it back into their mouths to chew the cud.

◀ *There are 14 million camels in the world and about 12.5 million of those are the one-humped dromedaries. They live mainly in Africa. Most Bactrian camels live in Asia, but they are critically endangered.*

115

Giraffes

🐾 **Giraffes are the tallest** mammals, growing to more than 5 m in height. This allows them to reach and eat the leaves, twigs and fruit at the very tops of trees.

🐾 **A giraffe's legs** are almost 2 m long.

▼ Giraffes evolved their long necks so they were able to eat food that no other grazing animal could reach. The tallest giraffes were less likely to die of starvation.

- **A giraffe's neck** may be over 2 m long, but it only has seven vertebrae – the same number as a human's.

- **Giraffes live in Africa**, south of the Sahara, in bush country.

- **Their tongues** are so tough that they can wrap them around the thorns of thorn trees to grab twigs.

- **When drinking**, a giraffe has to spread its forelegs wide or kneel down to reach the water. This position makes it very vulnerable to attack by lions.

- **When giraffes walk**, they move the two legs on one side of their body, and then the two on the other side. They can run very fast on their incredibly long legs, and can actually gallop as fast as a racehorse.

- **A giraffe's coat has patches** of brown on cream, and every giraffe's pattern is unique. The reticulated giraffes of East Africa have triangular patches, but the South African Cape giraffes have blotchy markings.

- **During breeding time**, rival males rub their necks together and swing them from side to side. This is known as necking.

- **When newborn**, a baby giraffe is very wobbly on its legs and cannot stand up for at least half an hour.

Deer

🐾 **Deer and antelope** are four-legged, hooved animals. Along with cows, hippos and pigs, they belong to the group called artiodactyls – animals with an even number of toes on each foot.

🐾 **Deer and antelope** chew the cud like cows – they chew food again, after first partially digesting it in a special stomach.

🐾 **Deer have branching** antlers of bone on their heads, which drop off and grow again each year.

🐾 **Most deer species** live in the woods and grasslands of mild regions such as northern Europe and North America.

🐾 **Male deer are called** stags or bucks, females are called does or hinds and babies are fawns or calves.

🐾 **The moose or elk** grows antlers more than 2 m in width.

🐾 **Usually only stags** have antlers. The only female deer to have antlers are caribou (reindeer).

▶ The place where male fallow deer display their size and strength is called a lek. Males on a lek fight each other at mating time, and one male may fight up to ten times a day. Females visit leks to choose the best mates.

🐾 **Indian spotted chevrotains** are tiny deer that grow no more than 60 cm long. They live in Sri Lanka and have long canine teeth instead of antlers.

🐾 **One of the world's** most endangered deer is the Père David's deer of China. It became extinct in the wild in the 1930s but was later reintroduced into the wild, and its population is slowly recovering.

🐾 **Pronghorns are** deer-like mammals that live in America. They are some of the fastest mammals over a long distance, reaching top running speeds of 65 km/h. Large herds of 1000 pronghorn gather during the winter months.

Antelope

- **Most antelope species** live in herds in Africa. Many are fast and graceful, including the impala and Thompson's gazelle.

- **The horns on an** antelope's head last for its entire lifetime.

- **Antelope are more** closely related to cows than they are to deer.

- **Antelope are fast runners**, but many of them are also quite bouncy and able to jump to escape from danger.

- **Their style of leaping** is called 'pronking' and the champion pronker is the springbok, which can leap 4 m high.

▶ No one is sure why antelope such springboks pronk. It might confuse a predator that is chasing it, or it may help an antelope spot predators hiding in the long grass.

🐾 **Antelope usually live** in herds. When many animals are keeping alert for signs of danger they are more likely to detect predators lurking nearby.

🐾 **Female antelope** give birth in spring, or when the seasonal rains are due so there is plenty of food for the mother and her calves.

🐾 **One of the most endangered** of all antelope is the scimitar-horned oryx from the deserts of northern Africa. It has long, elegant horns.

🐾 **Gazelles are usually** fawn-coloured with white bellies. This colouring helps camouflage them in the dry grasslands of their African home.

🐾 **Saigas are the swiftest** of all gazelles and have reached top speeds of 80km/h, kicking up clouds of dust as they escape their predators.

🐾 **The four-horned antelope** lives in India and Nepal and is the only animal to grow four horns.

🐾 **Common wildebeest** gather in huge herds that can number more than 1.5 million animals.

▶ Dik-diks are small antelope, with a body length of just 50–70 cm. Males and females stay together for life but the males do not help to raise their young.

Elephants

🐾 **There are two main** kinds of elephant – the African elephant and the Asian elephant.

🐾 **African elephants** are the largest land animals, with some males growing to 4 m in height.

🐾 **Asian elephants are smaller**, and have smaller ears. They also have one 'finger' on the tips of their trunks while African elephants have two.

▼ *A herd of African elephants is headed by a female called the matriarch who is often the oldest and largest in the herd. She leads the way during a journey.*

DID YOU KNOW?
Elephants use their highly mobile trunks like snorkels when crossing deep rivers.

- **Elephants are very intelligent**, with the biggest brain of all land animals. They have good memories.

- **They make a wide range** of low rumbling sounds that carry for long distances. We can only hear about one third of the sounds that elephants make.

- **Elephants usually** live for about 70 years.

- **Female elephants** (cows) live with their calves and young males (bulls) in herds. Older bulls are solitary.

- **When males are ready to mate**, they are said to be in 'musth'. This is a dangerous time, as the males become aggressive towards one another.

- **During musth**, glands between the males' eyes and ears produce an oozing substance, warning other males that they are in a fighting mood.

- **In dry areas**, herds may travel vast distances to find food. The bigger elephants protect the little ones between their legs.

Dugongs and manatees

▲ *A dugong grows up to 4 m long, including its tail. A female gives birth to just one calf at a time, and the youngster stays with her for up to 18 months while it learns the best places to find food.*

DID YOU KNOW?
Elephants are probably the closest living relatives of dugongs and manatees.

- **Dugongs live** in the southwest Pacific Ocean and the Indian Ocean.

- **Two types of manatees** live in the rivers of West Africa and the Amazon. The third lives in the Atlantic Ocean.

- **Dugongs and manatees** have to come to the surface every few minutes to breathe.

- **Manatees have only** six neck bones, unlike all other mammals, which have seven.

- **Manatees are sometimes** used to clear the weeds from tropical man-made reservoirs.

- **Dugongs feed on plants**, so they are also called sea cows. They sometimes swim long distances to feed.

- **Adult dugongs** have only a few peg-like teeth and use rough pads in their mouths to grind up food.

- **Unlike manatees**, the tail of the dugong is fluked, resembling that of whales and dolphins.

- **A dugong may live** for up to 70 years, but a female dugong will produce only five or six calves during her long lifetime.

Baleen whales

- **Whales, dolphins and porpoises** are large mammals called cetaceans that live mostly in the seas and oceans.

- **There are two types** of whale: toothed whales and baleen whales.

- **Like all mammals**, whales have lungs, so they have to come to the surface to breathe every 10 minutes or so, although they can stay down for 40 minutes, or longer.

- **Baleen whales** have a comb of thin plates called baleens in place of teeth. They feed by straining small creatures through their baleens.

- **Their diet includes** shrimp-like krill as well as other crustaceans and small fish. Grey whales also eat starfish and worms that they scoop up from the seabed.

- **There are four baleen** whale groups: right whales, pygmy right whales, grey whales and rorquals.

- **Bowhead whales** have the largest baleens of any whale. Each baleen plate measures 4–5 m long.

DID YOU KNOW?
Male humpbacks sing elaborate 'songs' lasting 20 minutes or more – perhaps to attract females.

- **Rorquals have grooves** on their throats and include humpback, minke and blue whales.

- **Baleen whales** go on incredible journeys across the oceans to reach the best feeding places throughout the year.

- **Humpbacks** make 'nets' out of streams of bubbles of air. They use these to catch shoals of small fish.

▲ *A humpback whale grows up to 19 m long and can weigh as much as 36 tonnes. Females are bigger than males. Whales sometimes pop their heads out of water just to look around. This is called spy-hopping.*

Whales keep in touch with each other using sounds called phonations. Large baleen whales make sounds that are too low for humans to hear, but they can be heard by other whales at least 80 km away.

Blue whales

- **Blue whales** are the largest creatures to have ever lived. They are baleen whales.

- **These giants grow** to be over 30 m in length and weigh more than 150 tonnes. Weighing a live blue whale is impossible, so weights are estimated.

- **They are gentle animals** that feed only on tiny creatures. In summer, they eat over 4 tonnes of krill every day – that's around four million krill.

▼ *A blue whale spouts from its blowholes, on the top of its head. The blowholes are nostrils and the spout is actually the whale breathing out, rather than a jet of water.*

- **A blue whale's tongue** is the same size as an elephant but they do not appear to have a particularly good sense of taste.

- **The part of a blue whale's brain** that processes sound is unusually large, and their sense of hearing is incredible.

- **Although blue whales** are the loudest animals in the world the sounds they make are very low frequency; too low for us to hear.

- **They may call to one** another to pass information about where the best blooms of krill are to be found.

- **Blue whale mothers** are pregnant for about a year. Their babies are over 7 m in length and weigh about 2.5 tonnes at birth.

- **When a blue whale** gulps water and krill its throat swells to four times its normal size.

- **During the summer**, blue whales feed in the icy waters around the Arctic and Antarctic where massive blooms of billions of krill can be found.

- **As winter approaches** the whales travel north to warmer, tropical seas. They scarcely feed during the winter, relying on stores of body fat to survive.

- **It is thought that blue whales** could live to be 100 years old, or more.

- **Some populations of blue whales** were totally wiped out when humans began hunting them in large numbers. Today, their numbers are slowly recovering.

Toothed whales

- **There are only 14 species** of baleen whale, but there are more than 70 species of toothed whales. This group includes dolphins and porpoises.

- **Toothed whales,** such as the sperm whale and the orca, or killer whale, have teeth and prey on large fish and seals.

- **The six groups of toothed whale** are sperm whales, beaked whales, belugas and narwhals, dolphins, porpoises and river dolphins.

- **The teeth of a toothed whale** are all the same shape: conical. It is a good shape for holding onto slippery fish.

- **Whales breathe through** blowholes on top of their heads. Baleen whales have two blowholes but toothed whales have just one.

- **When a whale breathes out**, it spouts out water vapour and mucus. When it breathes in, it sucks in about 2000 l of air within about two seconds.

- **A sperm whale** can hold its breath for two hours as it dives into the ocean's dark depths in search of deep-sea squid and fish.

- **Most toothed whales** live in small groups called pods.

- **Killer whales** are large dolphins. They are intelligent animals that work together to hunt in a pack.

- **Like land mammals**, whales nurse their babies with their own milk. Whale milk is rich – more than 50 percent fat – so babies grow fast.

- **Cuvier's beaked whales** dive to depths of 2000 m and suck squid into their mouths. Males have just two teeth and the females often have none.

A toothed whale's head contains an organ called the melon. The whale makes clicks that pass through the melon and bounce off a potential victim. When the sounds echo back to the whale it uses information from the echo to work out its prey's position and size.

▼ Sperm whales have huge heads that measure as much as 6 m long. The head contains the spermaceti organ, which helps a whale find food and communicate in deep water.

Dolphins and porpoises

- **Dolphins and porpoises** are small toothed whales. There are two kinds of dolphin: marine dolphins (36 species) and river dolphins (four species).

- **Dolphins have beak-like snouts** while porpoises have round heads with no 'beak'.

- **These small cetaceans** are mostly fast swimmers, and often leap out of the water as they swim.

- **Orcas**, or killer whales, are the largest dolphins and have a characteristic black-and-white pattern.

- **The Yangtze river dolphin** has probably been driven to extinction by harmful fishing methods, dams across rivers and pollution of river water.

- **Dolphins can see** equally well underwater and in air, unlike most other animals, although they do not see in colour.

- **They do not** have a sense of smell.

▼ Bottlenose dolphins live in warm seas and they usually hunt fish close to shore.

- **Bottle-nosed dolphins** get their name from their short beaks, which also make them look like they are smiling. They are friendly and often swim near boats.

- **Dolphins use sound** to find things and can identify different objects even when blindfolded.

- **Dolphins have their** own signature whistles which they use just like human names, to call each other undersea.

- **They communicate** with high-pitched clicks called phonations. Some dolphin clicks are higher than any other animal noise and humans are not able to hear them.

- **Hector's dolphins**, harbor porpoises and vaquitas are the smallest cetaceans of all. They are less than 2 m long.

- **Although most dolphins** and porpoises live in the oceans, some have taken up a life in fresh water. River dolphins are usually small, and often live in very polluted rivers where they compete with humans for food.

- **Ganges river dolphins** are almost blind.

Seals and sea lions

🐾 **Seals, sea lions and walruses** are sea mammals that mainly live in water and are agile swimmers, but which waddle awkwardly when they emerge onto land.

🐾 **Most seals eat fish**, squid and shellfish. Crabeater seals eat mainly shrimp-like krill, not crabs.

🐾 **Both seals and sea lions** have ears, but only sea lions, which includes fur seals have ear flaps.

🐾 **Only sea lions** can move their back flippers under their body when travelling about on land.

▶ Weddell seals live in the cold ocean around the Antarctic. They grow 2–3.5 m long and have a thick layer of blubber (fat) to keep them warm.

DID YOU KNOW?
The 4-m-long leopard seal of Antarctica feeds on penguins and even other seals.

▲ *There are seven species of sea lion. The males are always bigger than females, and often paler in colour. Males fight one another to protect their territory, and stop other males from mating with females.*

🐾 **When seals come ashore** to breed, they live for weeks in vast colonies called rookeries.

🐾 **Walruses are bigger** and bulkier than seals, and they have massive tusks and face whiskers.

🐾 **They use their tusks** to haul themselves out of the water and to break breathing holes in ice from below.

🐾 **Elephant seals are named** after the huge swollen noses of the males, which look like elephant trunks. The males use this nose like a loudspeaker to roar at rivals in the breeding season. Male elephant seals are up to ten times heavier than females.

🐾 **There are freshwater seals** in Lake Baikal in Russia.

Birds

What are birds?

- **There are currently** over 10,000 bird species.

- **Birds are the only living animals** that have feathers. (Some dinosaurs also had feathers.)

- **Wrens have 1000 feathers**, while swans have 20,000.

- **Birds have three** main kinds of feather: flight feathers on the wings and tail, body feathers to cover the body, and fluffy down feathers for warmth.

- **A bird's bones** are full of holes that keep them both lightweight and strong.

- **Flight feathers** are made of strands called barbs, which hook together. If the hooks come apart, they can be repaired easily, like doing up a zip.

- **Instead of teeth**, birds have a hard beak or bill. The size and shape of a bird's bill depends mainly on what it eats and where it finds its food.

- **Birds lay eggs** instead of giving birth to babies. The chicks that hatch out of the eggs may be independent (such as ducks, geese and chickens) or helpless (such as sparrows and starlings).

🐾 **Like mammals**, birds are warm-blooded – they keep their bodies at the same warm temperature all the time.

🐾 **Nearly half of the world's** birds go on special journeys called migrations to find food, water or nesting places, or to avoid bad weather.

▼ The Arctic tern is the champion bird migrant, flying from one end of the world and back again every year.

DID YOU KNOW?

Birds evolved from dinosaurs. Some fossils of feathered dinosaurs are more than 120 million years old.

Eggs and nests

DID YOU KNOW?

Cuckoos lay their eggs in the nests of other birds. The other birds then raise the chick as their own.

▲ *Perched in a tree, a nest can be a safe place for chicks. They are hidden from view of predators while their parents search for food.*

- **All birds reproduce** by laying hard-shelled eggs.

- **Birds that lay eggs** in the open usually lay camouflaged eggs. Birds that nest in holes or burrows, such as owls or kingfishers, usually lay white eggs.

- **A set of eggs** laid at a single time by one bird is called a clutch. The grey partridge can lay up to 16 eggs in a single clutch.

- **Most birds build** nests to lay their eggs in – usually bowl-shaped and made from twigs, grass and leaves.

- **The biggest nest** is that of the Australian mallee fowl, which builds a mound of soil 5 m across, with egg-chambers filled with rotting vegetation to keep it warm.

- **The weaverbirds** of Africa and Asia are very sociable. Some work together to weave huge, hanging nests, with scores of chambers, each with its own entrance.

- **Ovenbirds of Central** and South America are so-called because their nests look like the clay ovens made by local people. Some ovenbird nests can be 3 m in height.

- **Flamingos nest on lakes**, building mud nests that look like upturned sandcastles poking out of the water. They lay one or two eggs on top.

- **The edible nest swiftlet** builds its nest out of its own saliva, which hardens like cement. Some people collect these nests to make 'bird's nest soup'.

▲ Birds sit on their eggs to keep them warm, so the chicks inside can grow (this is called incubating the eggs). Flamingos and other birds that live in warm countries do not need to spend so much time incubating their eggs.

Flight

🐾 **The forelimbs** of birds have evolved into wings.

🐾 **The 'arm' bones** connect large muscles to the keel (a protruding bone in the middle of a bird's chest) and provide the power needed for flight.

🐾 **Feathers are essential** for birds to fly. They are made of keratin, the same substance that is present in reptile scales.

🐾 **Birds had feathered reptile** ancestors that lived at the time of the dinosaurs. Feathers kept them warm and might have been used to fly.

1 Arm bones
2 Keel
3 Wing feathers
4 Chest muscles
5 Tail feathers

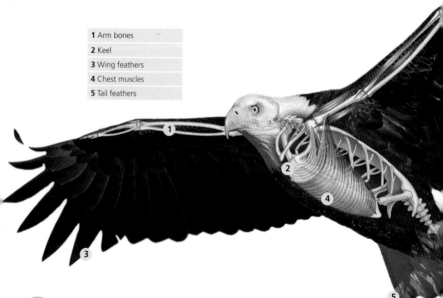

🐾 **Birds have to keep** their bodyweight down in order to fly. They have unusually strong but light skeletons with hollow bones.

🐾 **A bird's body** should be streamlined to fly fast. This means it is the right shape for moving through air without creating too much drag – a force that slows it down.

🐾 **The forked tail** of a frigatebird, swallow or kite enables the bird to change direction quickly while in the air.

🐾 **When a bird beats** its wings and moves forwards air flows over the top of the wings faster than it flows under the wings. This difference in air speed creates a difference in pressure, which allows the bird to rise.

🐾 **Large birds**, such as some birds of prey, rely on warm air currents (thermals) to fly. That is why they are less active in the morning when the air is still cool and there are few thermals.

🐾 **Birds with large wings** are able to soar on thermals, travelling great distances on the moving warm air and saving energy.

◀ *The American bald eagle has a wingspan of up to 2.5 m. These huge birds of prey are superb flyers that can swoop and soar, twist and turn in the sky. A male and female pair often perform acrobatic courtship dances during flight.*

Flightless birds

🐾 **Some birds are so good** at swimming or running that they do not need to fly. Flightless birds include big birds such as ostriches, emus and rheas, as well as penguins and a few unusual birds that live on islands, such as kiwis.

🐾 **The ostrich is the biggest** living bird, up to 2.75 m in height and weighing over 150 kg.

🐾 **To escape a lion**, the ostrich can hurtle over the African savannah grasslands at speeds of 70 km/h – as fast as a racehorse. Even when the ostrich tires, its strong legs can still deliver a massive kick in self defence.

🐾 **Ostriches have only** two toes on each foot – unlike the rhea of South America, which has three.

Cassowary

Ostrich

🐾 **The ostrich lays** the largest egg of any bird.

🐾 **The kiwi of New Zealand** is no bigger than a chicken. It has fur-like feathers and is the only bird with nostrils located at the tip of its bill, which it uses to sniff out worms and grubs.

🐾 **The rare kakapo parrot** of New Zealand lost the power of flight over time because it had no natural predators – until Europeans introduced dogs and cats to New Zealand.

🐾 **Rheas are probably** related to ostriches and emus but they live on the grasslands of South America. These flightless birds all have a similar lifestyle and are able to run fast across grasslands.

🐾 **The flightless** Galápagos cormorant uses its small wings to help it balance on the rocky islands of its home.

◄ *The plumage (feathers) of large flightless birds are of no use in flight but, like fur, they can help the animal keep warm and their colour may provide some camouflage.*

Emu

DID YOU KNOW?
The biggest bird ever is now extinct. The flightless elephant bird of Madagascar was truly gigantic, growing up to 4.5 m tall (taller than two grown men).

145

Penguins

- **There are 17 different** species of penguins, from gentoos, chinstraps and kings to emperors, rockhoppers and macaroni penguins.

- **Penguins spend three quarters** of their lives in the cooler parts of the southern oceans, only coming to land or sea ice in order to breed. Most penguins nest in huge colonies called rookeries.

- **Penguins cannot fly** but they are superb swimmers, using their flippers to 'fly' underwater and their tails and feet for steering and braking.

- **Penguin feathers** are waterproofed with oil and thick fat so they can survive in temperatures as low as −60°C.

- **The smallest penguin species** is the fairy penguin, at just 40 cm in height.

▼ Penguins, such as this king penguin, must find all of their food in the ocean. They mostly hunt fast-moving fish, squid and crustaceans (small shelled animals including krill).

- **Penguins can leap** high out of the water to land on an ice bank, but on land they can only waddle clumsily or toboggan along on their bellies.

- **Adélie penguins** waddle up to 100 km across the ice every year to reach their breeding ground.

DID YOU KNOW?
Some penguins dig burrows to nest in. A burrow is a safe place to lay an egg.

▶ Chinstrap penguins live near the Antarctic, breeding in huge colonies along coasts. Parents regurgitate (vomit) food for their chicks to eat, until the chicks lose their fluffy feathers and can hunt for themselves.

147

Emperor penguins

- **The emperor penguin** is the biggest swimming bird, at up to 1.2 m tall and weighing over 40 kg. This is twice the weight of any flying bird.

- **They can dive briefly** to depths of 250 m or more, and can hold their breath for up to 22 minutes while they dive in search of fish, krill and squid.

- **Emperor penguins** are able to cope with less oxygen than other diving birds, and are able to store it in their body.

- **They spend their whole lives** in the Antarctic and the surrounding seas.

- **Emperors are able to survive** winter on the world's coldest land, where there is a permanent blanket of snow and ice.

- **A male looks after his egg** for 100–120 days while the female returns to the sea to feed. The male doesn't eat during this time.

- **Males endure temperatures** as low as –50°C and freezing winds.

- **When a chick hatches** from its egg it can feed on fatty 'milk' that its father makes in its throat.

▼ *During the coldest times, penguins huddle together to share their body warmth. The adults take it in turns to be on the outside of a huddle, where the biting wind is at its worst. A group of huddling chicks is called a crèche.*

When females return from their trip to the sea they regurgitate food for the growing chicks to eat.

The main predators of emperor penguins are orcas, leopard seals and giant petrels, which snatch chicks from the ice.

Adult emperor penguins can go on trips of 1000 km to get food and return to their mate and chick.

Penguin chicks have soft, grey, fluffy feathers. They cannot swim until their adult plumage of black and white feathers grows in.

It is so cold that if a chick is left alone on the Antarctic ice it will die within two minutes. Only one in five chicks survives its first year of life.

▼ Penguin chicks look different from their parents. This might help the parents to recognise their own chicks, and encourages them to be gentle with the younger members of the colony.

DID YOU KNOW?

The male emperor penguin keeps the female's egg warm on his feet until it hatches.

149

Albatrosses, shearwaters and petrels

- **The wandering albatross** has the biggest wingspan of any bird – 3.5 m across.

- **Albatrosses can live** for 60, or even 80 years.

- **A wandering albatross** can reach speeds of almost 90 km/h. It glides without flapping its wings, and can cover thousands of kilometres in a day.

- **Most birds lay more** than one egg at a time, but albatrosses lay only one egg each year.

- **Of the 22 species** of albatross, 18 are threatened with extinction. They are being killed by longlining, a type of fishing that pulls the birds underwater so they drown.

- **A wandering albatross** chick spends nearly 10 months in its nest before it grows all its adult feathers.

▶ Black-browed albatrosses soar above the Southern Ocean, breeding on the many islands there. Some, however, have been found as far north as Scotland, proving just how far they can fly.

▶ Albatrosses nest in treeless places so they must build their nests on the ground or on rocky cliffs. Some albatrosses dig burrows in the soft ground. Chicks are fed with a liquid fat called stomach oil made in the parent's body.

🐾 **Giant petrels of Antarctica** use their powerful, hooked bills for feeding on dead animals and killing prey, such as penguins and albatrosses.

🐾 **Short-tailed shearwaters** breed on islands near Tasmania but for the rest of the year the adults fly about 32,000 km, around the whole of the Pacific Ocean.

🐾 **The storm petrel** is the smallest European seabird. It flutters above the waves, picking up fish and plankton from the surface.

🐾 **Diving petrels dive** into the sea and use their short wings to 'fly' underwater in search of prey, such as fish.

DID YOU KNOW?
When some seabirds are scared they simply squeak loudly and vomit at their attacker!

151

Gulls and waders

- **Gulls are big seabirds** that live on coasts all around the world, nesting on cliffs, islands or beaches.

- **They are related** to skuas and terns. Terns are smaller, more graceful birds than gulls, and have forked tails.

- **The great black-backed gull** is a fierce predator, feeding on a wide variety of prey, from fish to rabbits.

- **Herring gull chicks** peck at the red spot on their parents' bills to make them regurgitate (vomit) food for them to eat.

- **The ivory gull** is the only gull with completely white feathers. It lives mainly on Arctic coasts and islands.

▼ Herring gulls are adaptable birds, willing and able to eat almost anything they find. It takes four years for a chick to grow all of its adult feathers.

DID YOU KNOW?
Red knots are wading birds that migrate up to 12,000 km a year to breed in the best places.

◄ Male and female ringed plovers look almost identical, and share the care of eggs, which are are laid among pebbles and shingle at the coast.

🐾 **The pied avocet** uses its pointed, upturned bill to sweep through water or mud in search of food.

🐾 **A ringed plover** will lead predators away from its nest by pretending to have an injured wing.

🐾 **Female phalaropes** are more brightly coloured than the males. They leave the camouflaged males to take care of their eggs and rear the young.

🐾 **The woodcock** is an unusual wader because it lives in woodland instead of along the shoreline. Its mottled brown feathers provide good camouflage.

🐾 **In the breeding season**, groups of male ruffs gather at 'leks', places where they show off their remarkable head and neck feathers. This helps them to attract females.

153

Pelicans and cormorants

🐾 **Pelicans and cormorants** have webs of skin between all four of their toes. So do their relatives, the gannets and frigatebirds.

🐾 **Pelicans and their relatives** all feed on fish. Most of them live at sea and are strong fliers.

🐾 **The Australian pelican** has the longest bill of any bird. It can be up to 47 cm in length. The yellow or pink throat pouch becomes a scarlet red colour during courtship. Baby Australian pelicans may climb into their parents' pouches to feed on food their parents have regurgitated.

🐾 **The great white pelican** usually fishes in groups, forming a circle that moves forwards to force fish into the centre.

▼ *Cormorants and some of their relatives have wettable feathers rather than waterproof ones. After a dive, these birds must spread their wings to dry them out.*

▶ *Great white pelicans have a characteristic blue bill with a red stripe. They have huge wings and a wingspan of up to 3.6 m.*

Pelicans scoop up fish in their enormous throat pouches. A pelican's pouch expands to hold more food than its stomach.

Brown pelicans dive into the water from heights of 3–10 m above the surface. As they enter the water, they open their bills to trap fish in their throat pouches.

A cormorant's feathers soak up water easily, helping the bird to dive underwater to catch fish.

The magnificent frigatebird is named after the pirate ships called frigates because it steals food from other birds, like pirates steal from other ships. These birds are excellent fliers, twisting and turning to catch food in mid-air.

To attract a mate, a male frigatebird puffs out his red throat pouch like a balloon. Frigatebirds build a flimsy stick nest and the female lays one egg, which both parents incubate until it hatches. The chick can fly when it is 4–5 months old.

> **DID YOU KNOW?**
> Great white pelicans nest in colonies near water, forming groups of between 1000 and 30,000 pairs.

Cranes and rails

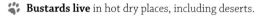

- **Cranes belong** to a group of birds that includes bustards, trumpeters, sun-bitterns and rails such as coots and moorhens.

- **Most members** of the crane family have long, slender legs and wings with rounded tips.

- **Common moorhens** live in freshwater places. Their large feet are similar to a hen's, so they do not sink into marshy ground.

- **If coots have more chicks** than they can feed, they attack the chicks that beg for food. Eventually, the weaker chicks die and there are fewer mouths to feed.

- **Grey crowned cranes** are unusual members of the family because despite their size – up to 1.1 m tall – they can perch in trees.

- **Bustards live** in hot dry places, including deserts.

▲ Common moorhens have largely black stocky bodies. Females prefer to mate with small, fat males.

- **Sun-bitterns live** alongside streams and rivers in shady parts of the rainforest. Their plumage is patterned with mottled markings of creams and browns so they can hide from predators.

- **The kori bustard** is one of the heaviest flying birds with weights of 11–19 kg. It rarely flies, except when it is in danger.

- **Red-crowned**, or Japanese, cranes are seen as a symbol of good luck in eastern Asia. There are fewer than 3000 left in the wild.

🐾 **Members of the crane** family have long throats. This feature enables them to produce very loud sounds that can be heard over long distances.

🐾 **Limpkins are particularly** noisy birds of American swamps – their calls are a series of haunting 'screams'.

🐾 **Many cranes and rails** are struggling to survive because they live in wetlands – a type of habitat that is threatened with destruction.

▼ Male kori bustards can inflate their large throat pouches up to four times their normal size. This is part of their courtship display. It makes them more attractive to females.

Flamingos

- **Flamingos are tall**, long-legged wading birds with pinkish plumage.

- **There are six species**: Caribbean flamingo, greater flamingo, lesser flamingo, puna (James's) flamingo, Chilean flamingo and Andean flamingo.

- **The Caribbean flamingo** has the deepest pink colour.

- **Their diet includes** pink animals, such as krill, and algae, which contain pink pigments (colours) that are stored in the birds' feathers.

- **The nest is made** from mud and built on the ground. There is just one egg and both parents take care of the egg and the chick.

- **Flamingos live in** large groups called colonies.

- **They feed together** and even perform courtship 'dances' when hundreds of birds appear to be moving their heads and necks at the same time.

- **As a flamingo wades** through shallow water it stirs up the mud to disturb animals that live there, so it can feed on them.

- **Larger birds feed on** shelled animals, such as crustaceans and molluscs, and worms.

- **Smaller flamingos** feed on little creatures and algae – a type of plant that lives in water.

- **A flamingo feeds** by putting its head into the water, upside down, and sweeps its head from side to side.

- **It sucks water** into its mouth and passes it through bristles, which trap the small animals as the water flows out of the bill.

- **Lesser flamingos** live by sun-baked salt lakes in Africa. They feed on tiny algae that grow in the lakes. There is enough food to support colonies of more than one million birds.

▼ *Flamingos often feed in very salty water, where few other animals can survive. This means there is less competition for the food that is available.*

Ducks and geese

🐾 **Ducks, geese and swans** are known as waterfowl, and they all live on or near water. There are about 170 species in total and each group makes a different sound – ducks quack, geese honk and swans hiss.

🐾 **Waterfowl can float** for hours and have webbed feet for paddling along. On water they are graceful, but on land they waddle awkwardly, since their legs are set far back under their body for swimming.

🐾 **Ducks have flatter bills** and shorter necks and wings than swans. Males are called drakes, and females are called ducks or hens. Babies are called ducklings.

🐾 **Diving ducks** (such as the pochard, tufted duck and the scoter) dive for food such as roots, shellfish and insects on the river bed.

🐾 **Dabbling ducks** (such as the mallard, widgeon, gadwall and teal) dabble – they sift water through their beaks for food.

🐾 **Some dabblers feed** at the surface. Others up-end – sticking their heads into the water to sift out water weeds and snails from muddy water.

🐾 **Swans are the largest** waterfowl. They have long elegant necks and pure white plumage – apart from the black-neck swan of South America and the Australian black swan.

🐾 **Baby swans are** called cygnets and are mottled grey. Baby geese are called goslings.

🐾 **Most waterfowl feed** in water but geese feed on land, pulling up grass and other plants with their strong bills.

▼ Male teals have beautiful plumage, with chestnut heads and bright green eye patches. Females have dull brown plumage, which helps them hide from danger when they are nesting.

DID YOU KNOW?
Swans and geese both form lifelong partnerships with their mates and they usually share in the care of their young.

Herons, storks and spoonbills

◀ Shoebills use their powerful, hooked bills to capture large, strong prey and often bite off a fish's head before swallowing its body whole.

🐾 **Herons have slim bodies**, long legs, long necks and large, wide wings. There are about 60 species.

🐾 **Most herons feed** by wading into shallow water and stabbing fish or other creatures with their powerful bills.

🐾 **The black heron** shades the water with its outstretched wings when hunting. This reduces reflections, so it can see the fish more easily.

🐾 **Herons usually** nest in colonies called heronries. They build loose stick-nests in trees.

🐾 **Cattle egrets are** related to herons. They follow herds of grazing animals, and catch the insects they disturb.

🐾 **Shoebills are a type** of stork with a massive bill that helps them to catch the slippery lungfish on which they feed. Like other storks, shoebills clap the two halves of their bill together as a display or threat.

- **The white stork** lives in Eurasia in the summer, and migrates to Africa, India and southern China in the winter.

- **White storks build** twig-nests on roofs, and some people think they bring luck to the houses they nest on.

- **Spoonbills are named** after the shape of their bill, which is sensitive, allowing them to feel their prey moving in the water.

- **The sacred ibis** was held in high regard by the ancient Egyptians. It is common in tomb paintings and millions of mummified birds have been found.

▶ The blue heron is the largest heron in North America, standing over 1.5 m tall. These wading birds nest in tall trees.

Birds of prey

- **There are 319 species** of birds of prey. The group includes kestrels, falcons, goshawks, buzzards and vultures.

- **Most birds of prey** are hunters. They feed on other birds, fish and small mammals, catching their prey in their claws.

- **Most birds of prey** are strong fliers, with sharp eyes, powerful talons (claws) and a hooked bill.

- **Birds of prey** are active during the day, unlike owls, which hunt at night-time.

- **Eagles are the most** powerful birds of prey. Female harpy eagles from the Amazon rainforest are strong enough to snatch monkeys and sloths from the treetops.

▶ Ospreys are also known as fish hawks. They have rough spines on their talons that help them to grip tightly on to wet, wriggling fish.

◄ *Peregrine falcons hunt other birds, which they catch in flight. These agile birds are found on all continents except Antarctica, and are one of the most widespread of all bird species.*

🐾 **Birds of prey** have both strength and agility. The hobby is one of the most acrobatic flyers and can change direction fast enough to catch swallows and bats in mid-air.

🐾 **The snail kite** has an unusual diet – it feeds only on water snails! This kite's thin hooked bill reaches inside the snail's shell to pull out its body without even breaking the shell.

🐾 **In the Middle Ages**, merlins and falcons were trained to fly from a falconer's wrist to catch birds and animals.

DID YOU KNOW?

The peregrine falcon can reach speeds of 200–250 km/h when stooping (diving) on prey.

165

Bald eagles

🐾 **Bald eagles are large** birds of prey that live in North America. They are the USA's national symbol.

🐾 **These birds are named** after the white feathers on their heads – an old meaning of the word 'bald' is 'white'.

🐾 **They are found in** many habitats but prefer to stay close to rivers or the sea. Some birds migrate to avoid the worst winter weather.

🐾 **These raptors are** adaptable birds and eat a range of food. They hunt rodents, birds and fish, and also carrion (dead animals).

🐾 **An adult bald eagle** is nearly one metre long, and has a wingspan of about 2.5 m.

🐾 **A male and female** bald eagle build a big, bulky nest together. It is called an eyrie and can be up to 4 m tall.

🐾 **The female lays** a clutch of two or three eggs and the parents share the care of the eggs and the chicks.

◀ *About 300 bald eagles migrate south to Arizona during the winter, finding plenty of fish in the rivers of the Grand Canyon.*

DID YOU KNOW?
A bald eagle's feathers weigh about 700 g, that's twice as much as its skeleton.

🐾 **It is estimated** that there are about 70,000 bald eagles, half of which live in the state of Alaska where there is a good supply of salmon.

🐾 **Young bald eagles** have black bills. They do not get the distinctive yellow bill and white head feathers until they are about five years old.

🐾 **When a bald eagle** gets too hot it perches and holds its wings away from its body, so it can lose the heat (birds do not sweat).

🐾 **They have excellent eyesight** and can see both to the front and the side at the same time.

🐾 **They have colour vision** and can focus on distant objects much better than humans can.

🐾 **The number** of bald eagles fell dramatically during the 20th century. Since the 1970s the populations have slowly recovered and the species has been saved from extinction.

Vultures

▲ *Like other large birds of prey, an Andean condor finds it hard to launch into flight from the ground. It is much easier to take off from a height.*

Vultures are the biggest birds of prey. They do not hunt, but feed on carrion.

The palm-nut vulture is the only plant-eating bird of prey and it feeds on palm oil nuts.

Vultures have broad wings, which they use to glide high on rising warm air currents, called thermals.

Egyptian vultures sometimes throw stones at ostrich eggs to break open the thick shells and feed on the contents.

🐾 **The Californian condor** is very rare. All the wild birds were captured in the mid 1980s, but some have since been bred in captivity and returned to the wild.

🐾 **Vultures are great fliers** and spend hours soaring, scanning the ground with their sharp eyes for food.

🐾 **King vultures** have a strong sense of smell, which helps them to find animal remains in their dense tropical forest habitat.

🐾 **The lammergeier** is known as the bearded vulture because it has a beard of black bristles on its chin.

🐾 **Lammergeiers fly to great** heights and drop animal bones onto rocks to smash them open. Then they feed on the nourishing marrow inside the bones.

▶ *In common with most other vultures, the strange-looking king vulture does not have a voice box, so the only sounds it can make are croaks, hisses and snorts. Both sexes grow lumps of orange flesh around the bill.*

169

Owls

- **Most owls are** night-time predators. They roost in trees during the day, so many owls have mottled brown feathers for camouflage.

- **There are two big families** of owl – barn owls and typical owls. Barn owls have a heart-shaped disc of feathers on the face, relatively small eyes and long, slim legs.

- **Typical owls** have enormous eyes set in a round disc of feathers on the face, and very large ears. There are 186 typical, or true owl species.

- **There are 15 species** of barn owl. The most widespread is the common barn owl, found everywhere but Antarctica.

🐾 **Small owls eat** mostly insects. Bigger owls eat mice and shrews. Eagle owls can catch young deer.

🐾 **In the country**, the tawny owl's diet is 90 percent small mammals, but many now live in towns where their diet is mainly small birds, such as sparrows and starlings.

◄ Snowy owls are perfectly camouflaged in their cold Arctic habitat. Males are mostly white, but females have dark marks that help them hide from view when they nest on the ground.

🐾 **Owls can hear** sounds that are ten times softer than those humans can hear, and are able to hunt in darkness by picking up the sounds made by their prey.

🐾 **Most birds' eyes** look out to the sides, but owls' eyes look straight forward like those of humans. This is probably why the owl has been a symbol of wisdom since ancient times.

🐾 **The flight feathers** on an owl's wings muffle the sound of its wingbeats so that it can swoop silently onto its prey.

🐾 **The white feathers** of snowy owls provide good camouflage in the wastes of the Arctic. These owls can swoop down on their prey, taking it by surprise.

Gamebirds

- 🐾 **Many gamebirds were** hunted for food or sport, which is how they got their name.

- 🐾 **Gamebirds spend most** of the time strutting along the ground looking for seeds. They fly only in emergencies.

- 🐾 **There are 290 species** of gamebird. These include pheasants, grouse, partridges, quails and peafowl.

- 🐾 **Most of the 48 species** of pheasant originated in China and central Asia.

◄ The California quail has a delicate, teardrop-shaped crest above its eyes. This bird is very territorial, and rarely leaves its home area.

DID YOU KNOW?
All farmyard turkeys are descended from the American wild turkey, which grows to 1.5 m.

🐾 **Many female gamebirds** (hens) have dull brown plumage that helps them to hide in their woodland and moorland homes.

🐾 **Many male gamebirds** (cocks) have very colourful plumage to attract mates.

🐾 **During the breeding season**, gamebird cocks strut and puff up their plumage to attract a mate. They also draw attention to themselves by cackling, whistling and screaming.

🐾 **Male pheasants often** fight each other violently to win a particular mating area.

🐾 **The jungle fowl** of Southeast Asia is the wild ancestor of the domestic chicken.

🐾 **Sandgrouse live in** the desert and male birds fly many kilometres to find water. They store water in their belly feathers and carry it back to their chicks.

▶ When a male greater sage grouse displays to females he fans his tail feathers and inflates special throat sacs, puffing himself up to look even bigger and more impressive.

Pigeons and doves

- **There are about 320 members** of the pigeon and dove family. Doves are usually smaller than pigeons.

- **These birds have small**, round heads and their bills are slim with a fleshy section near the base.

- **Pigeon bodies are plump** and covered with a dense layer of feathers, and their legs are short and scaly.

- **Members of the pigeon** family mostly eat plant material. Some of them have a diet of seeds while others – usually tropical species – eat fruit.

- **Most pigeons** and doves coo when they call.

- **A turtledove** is a little bigger than a blackbird and is regarded as one of the most beautiful birds in its family.

- **Although European pigeons** are mostly grey, their tropical cousins often have brightly coloured feathers.

- **Both parents make a fat-rich** substance in their crop (a pouch in the bird's digestive system). They feed this 'milk' to their chicks as they grow.

- **Pink pigeons** live only on the island of Mauritius. They are one of the world's rarest birds. At one time, their population dropped to just 20 birds.

▶ *The southern crowned-pigeon is a technicolour bird with a maroon breast, blue-grey feathers, red eyes and purple legs and feet. Its crowning glory is a fan of delicate, lacy grey feathers.*

Parrots and cockatoos

- **There are 375 or so parrot species** divided into three main groups – true parrots, cockatoos and New Zealand parrots.

- **Parrots are intelligent birds**. African grey parrots are able to understand shapes, colour and numbers and can work out some problems as well as a four-year-old child.

- **Typical parrots are** brightly coloured birds. They live in flocks in tropical forests, feeding on fruits, nuts and seeds.

- **Parrots have feet** with two toes pointing forwards and two backwards, allowing them to grip branches and hold food.

- **Cockatoos are the only** parrots with feathery head crests. They raise and lower their head crests when they are excited, frightened or angry.

- **The budgerigar is a small** parakeet from central Australia. It is very popular as a pet.

- **The hanging parrots** of Southeast Asia get their name because they sleep upside down like bats.

- **The kea of New Zealand** is a parrot that eats meat as well as fruit. It was once wrongly thought to be a sheep killer.

▶ Like many members of the parrot family, the colourful scarlet macaw is in danger of extinction. So many birds have been taken for the pet trade that the wild populations are close to total collapse.

- **Parrots are well known** for their mimicry of human voices. Some have a repertoire of 300 words or more.

- **The kakapo of New Zealand** is a rare parrot that lives on the ground and only comes out at night. It is the heaviest of all parrots and is too heavy to fly. In the breeding season, males advertise for mates with loud booming calls that can be heard up to one kilometre away.

DID YOU KNOW?

Parrots often pair for life, and they can live long lives – up to 80 years in some species.

Cuckoos and turacos

🐾 **Cuckoos and turacos** belong to a secretive group of birds that are shy and often very well camouflaged. There are about 170 species in this group.

🐾 **Common cuckoos** live throughout Europe and most of Asia. They migrate south to spend the winter in Africa.

🐾 **Some cuckoos are called** brood parasites. They lay their eggs in other birds' nests and leave the adoptive parents to feed their chicks.

🐾 **Cuckoo chicks throw** any other eggs out of the nest. This means their adoptive parents can devote all their time to just feeding the cuckoo chick.

🐾 **The cuckoo is named** after its 'coo-koo' song. Most cuckoos and turacos have loud voices.

▼ *A cuckoo chick is always hungry, and soon grows bigger than the adult that is caring for it.*

- **Hoatzins have an extra-large** stomach that helps them to digest their diet of leaves.

- **Hoatzins live in** northern parts of South America and they can grow to 70 cm long. Young birds have tiny claws on their wings, rather like prehistoric birds did.

- **Turacos have short**, rounded wings and long tails. They often have brightly coloured feathers.

- **Feathers get their colour** from substances called pigments. Turacos have green and red pigments that are not found in any other type of bird.

- **Roadrunners are long-tailed**, large members of the cuckoo family that spend most of their time on the ground.

- **Roadrunners live** in the desert and chase small animals such as lizards and snakes. They are able to fly, but they are swift runners with top speeds of about 30 km/h.

▲ A pair of hoatzins build their nest in a tree near water, and guards their territory from any other birds.

179

Nightjars and frogmouths

- **These birds are mostly** nocturnal, which means they are more active at night than in the daytime.

- **Nightjars and their** relatives have large heads, long bodies and long wings. Their feathers are coloured and patterned to blend into their woodland homes.

- **Potoos live in** Central and South America. A potoo avoids predators to by pretending to be a branch during the day and can sit perfectly still for hours at a time.

▼ *The large-tailed nightjar lives in Southeast Asia, from India to the coastal forests of Eastern Australia. These birds feed on moths and other flying insects.*

🐾 **Oilbirds are the only** nocturnal birds that survive on a diet of fruit. During the day, they hide out in caves.

🐾 **Most members** of the oilbird family are swift movers and can change direction easily when flying. They have weak legs and feet and move clumsily on the ground.

🐾 **Nightjars and some** of their relatives have stiff little bristles around their beaks. Experts are unsure of their purpose.

🐾 **A tawny frogmouth** has large eyes to help it see in the dark. It jumps on its prey, such as insects and spiders.

🐾 **Poorwills are named** after their song, which sounds like 'poor-will, poor-will, poor-will'.

🐾 **Male standard-winged** nightjars have two extra-long wing feathers that measure up to 75 cm long.

🐾 **European nightjars are** acrobatic fliers and can catch insects as they swoop through the air.

▶ *A Hodgson's frogmouth and its chicks are perfectly camouflaged in a tree. A large mouth enables this bird to eat big prey, such as frogs.*

181

Swifts and hummingbirds

- **Swifts and hummingbirds** have tiny feet and legs, spending most of their time on the wing. They only use their feet to perch when breeding or roosting.

- **Swifts glue their nests** together with sticky saliva from special salivary glands.

- **Their short**, gaping bills allow swifts to catch insects while flying.

- **Swifts may fly** through the night, and even sleep on the wing. European swifts will fly all the way to Africa and back to Europe without stopping.

▲ The crimson topaz is a hummingbird of the Amazon rainforest and one of the largest hummingbirds in Brazil. A male's long tail feathers cross each other.

◀ White-throated needletails are swifts that can reach phenomenal speeds when flying. They are thought to be one of the fastest birds in the world, and probably reach speeds greater than 110 km/h.

🐾 **The fragile nest** of the crested tree swift is only about 2.5 cm across and has a single egg that is glued inside with saliva. The parents will take it in turns to incubate the egg.

🐾 **Great dusky swifts** nest and roost behind waterfalls, and have to fly through the water to get in and out.

🐾 **Hummingbirds are tiny**, bright, tropical birds that sip nectar from flowers. There are around 340 species.

🐾 **They are the most amazing** aerial acrobats, hovering and twisting in front of flowers.

🐾 **The bee hummingbird** is the world's smallest bird – including its long bill, it measures just 5 cm.

DID YOU KNOW?
When hovering, horned sungem hummingbirds beat their wings 90 times per second.

Kingfishers, bee-eaters and hornbills

- **Kingfishers belong** to a varied group of birds, which also includes rollers, hoopoes, bee-eaters and hornbills. Many of these birds are brightly coloured, with large bills.

- **They nest in tunnels**, often in riverbanks but also in tree holes or termite nests.

- **The laughing kookaburra** is a giant kingfisher named for its loud call, which sounds like a person chuckling.

- **Rollers are named** for the male's rolling courtship flight. He flies high up in the air and then dives down, somersaulting through the air as he falls.

- **The hoopoe is named** for its call, which sounds like 'hoo-poo-poo'. It uses its long, curved bill to probe the ground for worms and insects.

◀ Kingfishers perch on branches over clear streams and rivers, watching for signs of fish swimming below. When they spot their prey, kingfishers move with lightning speed.

◀ A male hornbill brings his mate food so she can stay safe in the tree, keeping their eggs warm. This strategy means the eggs stay hidden and protected from predators until they hatch.

🐾 **Parent green wood hoopoes** have up to ten helpers. They gather food and defend the nest. When the chicks mature, they help the adults that raised them.

🐾 **Hornbills have a** horn-like casque on top of their bills. This may amplify their calls, making them louder.

🐾 **The rhinoceros hornbill** has a casque that turns up at the end, like a rhino's horn.

🐾 **Hornbills nest** in tree holes, which get sealed up with mud. The female stays inside the tree for three months while she incubates the eggs. The male passes her food through a small hole.

🐾 **Bee-eaters hold** bees or other stinging insects in their bills and beat or rub them against a perch to get rid of the poison from the sting. Then they can safely swallow the insect.

Woodpeckers and toucans

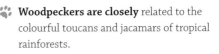

🐾 **Woodpeckers are closely** related to the colourful toucans and jacamars of tropical rainforests.

🐾 **They have two toes on** each foot pointing forwards and two pointing backwards. These help them cling to trees and branches.

🐾 **Woodpeckers chisel** into decaying tree trunks to search for insects. They use their long, sticky tongues to lick up any insects that they find.

🐾 **Acorn woodpeckers** drill holes in trees and wedge acorns in them tightly so that squirrels cannot steal them.

🐾 **Woodpeckers claim** their territory not by singing, but by hammering their bills against trees.

◀ *Greater spotted woodpeckers live in European and north Asian woodlands, although they sometimes visit parks and gardens. Males and females look similar, but males have red feathers on the back of the head.*

◄ The toco toucan is the largest member of the toucan family, at about 60 cm long. The bird appears to have a blue eye, but it actually has a circle of blue skin around a black eye.

DID YOU KNOW?
When toucan chicks hatch from their eggs they are completely naked, with no downy feathers.

🐾 **Instead of feeding** in trees, green woodpeckers feed mainly on the ground.

🐾 **There are about** 40 species of toucan. They live in the forests of Central and South America.

🐾 **They usually eat fruit**, but they also prey on insects, lizards and eggs from other birds' nests.

🐾 **No one knows why** toucans have such large bills. A big bill may enable a bird to reach fruit at the tips of branches, and it may help toucans control their body temperature.

Passerines

- **Passerines are** perching birds that are able to hold tightly to slender branches.

- **There are about** 6000 passerines, so this group makes up two-thirds of all birds. They are found all over the world.

- **Most passerines sing** complex songs. Each species has its own song, which it learns when it is a chick.

- **Some birds are known** for their beautiful songs, for example, larks, nightingales and thrushes.

- **Usually only male songbirds** sing – mainly in the mating season, to warn off rivals and attract females.

- **A passerine has four** toes on each foot. Three toes face forwards and the fourth toe faces backwards.

- **The toes work together** to grip. This means that a passerine can perch on very slim twigs and even grass stems.

- **A passerine's toes** are able to grip even when the bird is asleep.

- **Finches mostly feed** on seeds and they have evolved strong, short bills for cracking seeds open. They use their tongues to reach the soft kernel inside.

- **Tanagers are tropical passerines** with brightly coloured plumage. Like most other passerines, they build small cup-shaped nests in trees.

DID YOU KNOW?
The world's most common wild bird is the red-billed quelea. Billions of these passerines live in Africa.

- **The European robin** belongs to a large group of passerines called Old World flycatchers. Flycatchers eat insects and lay up to 11 eggs at a time.

- **Swallows and martins** are superb fliers and some species go on long migrations in search of food.

- **The crow family** of birds is thought to include the most developed and intelligent of all birds.

◀ The orange-red breast of a European robin makes this an easy bird to identify. Robins often set up their territories in gardens, and fiercely defend them from other robins. Both males and females have orange-red feathers.

189

Crows, jays and magpies

▶ *Rooks have no feathers around the base of the bill, so they are sometimes called 'bare-faced crows'. Rooks have excellent hearing.*

- **Crows and their relatives** are called corvids. This group includes ravens, rooks, jays, jackdaws, nutcrackers, choughs, magpies and treepies. They are passerines (perching birds).

- **Corvids are among** the most intelligent of all birds.

- **Corvids are medium-sized** birds with large, strong beaks and long legs.

- **Most crows have black feathers** but jays and magpies are often colourful.

- **Many corvids hide** their food when they have too much to eat in one go. They have excellent memories and can find stored food many months later.

- **Crows can learn** to recognise individual human faces.

- **Rooks live in large groups** called rookeries. Once they have chosen a mate they usually stay with their partner for life.

- **Magpies eat insects**, plants and carrion but they also attack chicks and rabbits, using their sharp-edged beaks to kill their prey.

- **Common ravens** are among the largest of all crows, with a body length of up to 65 cm. They are adaptable birds that can survive in many habitats, including the high slopes of Mount Everest.

- **Jackdaws can learn** how to 'sing' simple human words. They also call to each other to share food, or to warn their flock if predators are nearby.

Sparrows and starlings

The birds of the Old World sparrow family live in Europe, Asia and Africa. The 'sparrows' that live in the Americas belong to a different family.

Sparrows live in a large range of habitats, especially woodlands, deserts and grasslands.

Sparrows often make their homes close to humans, so they are common visitors to gardens where they feed on seeds and insects.

In general, sparrows are social animals and often roost in large groups especially where there is plenty of food.

Flocks of starlings are called murmurations and can contain as many as 100,000 birds.

Starlings are found throughout the world, in most habitats except deserts.

Starlings are small to medium-sized birds and many of them have shiny black plumage.

▶ The feathers of a European starling are a glossy mixture of blue-purple and deep green. The cream speckles often disappear on a male's plumage during the summer.

- **Members of the starling** family often have iridescent feathers – they have a metallic sheen and can be very colourful.

- **Insects and fruit** are the preferred foods of most starlings.

- **Red-billed oxpeckers** are unusual starlings that feed on insects and other pests that they find on the skin of large mammals such as rhinos. They also feed on the blood that oozes out of wounds on their skin.

- **Mynah birds are starlings** and, like other members of the family, they can learn new songs throughout their lives.

- **Mynahs are called mimics** because they are able to copy a range of sounds, even human speech.

▼ Sparrows usually breed in the spring, so their young will hatch when there is plenty of food available. Most species lay four or five eggs at a time.

Reptiles

What are reptiles?

- **Reptiles are vertebrates** (animals with a backbone) with scaly skin. Most of them lay eggs on land, although some snakes and lizards give birth to live young.

- **There are about 9400** different species of reptiles.

- **They are divided into** four groups: crocodilians (crocodiles, alligators and caimans), snakes and lizards, turtles and tortoises, and the tuataras.

- **Reptiles were the first** large creatures to live entirely on land, about 310–315 million years ago.

- **They are more common** in hot places but some reptiles live in water and a few species are able to survive in cool climates.

- **Reptiles are described** as cold-blooded. This means that, unlike birds and mammals, their body temperature is controlled by their surroundings.

- **Reptiles bask in the sun** to warm up their bodies before they can be very active.

- **A reptile's skin has** overlapping scales that are made of a horny substance called keratin.

- **Keratin can be coloured**, and many reptiles have colours and patterns that either warn other animals to stay away, or help them to hide in their habitat.

- **There are just two species** of tuatara. They look like lizards but there are important differences between the two groups, including the shape of their skulls.

🐾 **Tuataras belong to** a group of reptiles that walked the Earth about 200 million years ago – at the same time as their relatives, the dinosaurs. Today they live only on small islands near New Zealand.

🐾 **Unlike most other reptiles**, tuataras are nocturnal and can forage for insects at night, even when the temperature drops to 10°C.

🐾 **Many reptiles rest under** leaves or rocks or in burrows, where they can stay safe at night, or during cooler times of year.

▼ *Collared lizards are common in warm habitats of North America. They lead typical reptile lives – basking in the sun, eating insects and laying eggs in burrows.*

Lizards

- **Lizards make up a large**, successful group of about 5500 species. They live in many parts of the world and in a variety of habitats.

- **They are mostly** small animals with four legs and a long tail.

- **Lizards move in many ways** – running, scampering and slithering. Some can glide between trees. Unlike mammals, their limbs stick out sideways rather than downwards.

- **Most lizards lay eggs**, although a few give birth to their young. Unlike birds or mammals, a mother lizard does not nurture (look after) her young.

- **The basilisk lizard** is also known as the Jesus Christ lizard because it can walk on water.

▶ Thorny devils are extraordinary, spiny lizards that can survive in the extreme habitat of the Australian desert. They only eat ants – feasting on up to 2500 in one meal.

🐾 **Some lizards** are able to shed their tails when they are chased. The predator is left holding onto a wriggling tail while the lizard escapes. The lizard usually grows a new tail.

🐾 **When threatened,** a chuckwalla runs into a rocky crevice and expands its body with air until it is jammed into the tiny space – so a predator cannot pull it out.

🐾 **The amphisbaenians** are very closely related to lizards, but they do not have legs. They are also known as 'worm lizards'. They burrow through soil looking for worms and insects.

🐾 **Lizards can live** in deserts because they only need a small amount of water to survive.

🐾 **A lizard has five clawed** toes on each foot. Web-footed geckoes have webbed feet so they can run across sand dunes without sinking.

DID YOU KNOW?

Most lizards live just a few years but a blue iguana called Godzilla died in 2004 – aged 59.

199

Iguanas

- **Iguanas are large lizards** that live mainly around the Pacific and in the Americas.

- **Unlike other lizards**, larger iguanas are plant eaters. Most eat flowers, fruit and leaves.

- **The common iguana** lives high up in trees, but lays its eggs in a hole in the ground.

- **When disturbed**, common iguanas will jump from heights of 10 m or so, from their homes in the branches into the water below. They then swim quickly away from danger.

- **The rhinoceros iguana** of the West Indies gets its name from the pointed scales on its snout.

- **The marine iguana** of the Galápagos Islands is the only lizard that spends much of its life in the sea.

- **Marine iguanas gather** together in large groups to sleep at night, which helps them to save energy and keep warm.

- **When in the water**, a marine iguana may dive for 15 minutes or more, pushing itself along with its tail.

- **Although marine iguanas** cannot breathe underwater, their heart rate slows so that they use less oxygen.

- **Marine iguanas** have an unusual diet. They feed on the seaweed growing on underwater rocks.

DID YOU KNOW?

Female iguanas often develop orange spots after mating. The spots deter males from pestering the females!

▲ Iguanas are often colourful, and many species even change their skin colour. A green iguana is larger than most lizards in this group, growing up to one metre long. Their green skin provides excellent camouflage in trees.

201

Chameleons

- **There are more than** 150 species of chameleon, most of which live on the island of Madagascar and in mainland Africa.

- **The smallest chameleon** could balance on your finger but the biggest, Oustalet's chameleon, is the size of a small cat.

- **A chameleon can look** forwards and backwards at the same time, as each of its amazing eyes can swivel in all directions independently of the other.

- **A chameleon's tongue** may be as long – or longer – than its body but is normally squashed up inside its mouth.

- **A chameleon shoots** out its tongue in a fraction of a second to trap its victim on a sticky pad at the tip.

- **The tongue is fired** out from a launching bone on the chameleon's lower jaw.

- **Most lizards can change colour**, but chameleons are experts, changing quickly to all sorts of colours.

- **Chameleons change** colour when they are angry or frightened, too cold or too hot, or sick. They sometimes change to match their surroundings.

◄ *Male panther chameleons are among the most colourful of all animals. Chameleons can wrap their tails around a branch, and their toes are a good shape for gripping tightly.*

The colour of a chameleon's skin is controlled by pigment cells called chromatophores, which change colour as they change size.

Chameleons feed on insects and spiders, hunting in trees by day.

203

Monitor and venomous lizards

- **Monitor lizards** and venomous lizards belong to a group of large lizards called anguimorphs.

- **There are about** 220 species of anguimorph and they prey on many animals, including slugs, snails and small mammals.

- **Slow worms** and glass lizards are legless and look more like snakes than lizards.

▲ *The large Gila monster (up to 50 cm long) is a slow mover in the heat, but becomes more active at the end of the day. Its bold colouring warns other animals that it has a deadly bite.*

- **Monitor lizards** are large, stocky reptiles that are most active in the daytime. They have forked tongues, which they use to 'taste' the air and locate food.

- **Many monitors hunt**, but they also feed on carrion.

- **Unlike snakes**, slow worms have eyelids that close. They can also shed their tails, like other lizards, when they are in danger.

- **The European glass lizard** grows to 1.2 m long.

- **Despite their size**, many monitor lizards are able to climb trees. Some species prefer to live near water and are good swimmers.

- **Gray's monitor lizards** eat snails and fruit, Dumeril's monitors swims in search of crabs, and green tree monitors eat insects and bird eggs.

- **There are two species** of venomous lizards that live in the southwest USA and Mexico: Gila monsters and Mexican beaded lizards. Both have venomous bites and attack rabbits, rodents, birds and other lizards. They also eat eggs.

- **A Gila monster** can eat a huge meal in one go. It stores the extra food as fat in its tail.

- **When a Mexican beaded lizard** bites its prey it grips on tightly while venom from its mouth flows into the bite wounds. The venom flows from special glands through grooves in the teeth on the lizard's lower jaw.

Komodo dragon

The heaviest lizards in the world are a type of monitor lizard found only on a small group of islands in Indonesia. They are called Komodo dragons, after one of the islands.

A wild Komodo dragon is 2–3 m long and weighs about 70 kg.

These large lizards live in dry forests, grasslands and on beaches. Young Komodos spend the first months of their lives hiding in trees to avoid being eaten by the adults.

A Komodo dragon is a fast, powerful beast with strong legs and a large muscular tail. Its jaws contain glands that produce venom, as well as being lined withlined with sharp, serrated teeth.

When a Komodo bites its prey, venom seeps into the wounds caused by its teeth. If the prey escapes it will soon die from its venom-filled wounds, and the Komodo dragon will find it and eat it.

Males fight one another when it is mating time. Once mating has taken place, a female digs a hole and lays up to 25 eggs in it. After covering the nest with soil and leaves, the female lies on top of it to keep it warm.

When a young Komodo hatches from its egg it is already nearly 40 cm long.

When Komodos kill they must tear chunks of flesh off their victim because they cannot chew.

▶ *Komodo dragons usually live alone but they sometimes gather in a group when they are following the scent of food.*

- **Komodos chase** and kill other animals to eat, although they most often eat carrion.

- **They attack large mammals** including pigs, deer, water buffalo, goats, other lizards – and sometimes even humans.

- **A Komodo uses** its long forked tongue to taste the chemicals in the air, similar to the way that other animals smell things.

207

Geckos

- **Geckos are some** of the most familiar of lizards because they often live close to humans.

- **They are nocturnal hunters** that mostly eat insects and spiders.

- **A gecko can easily** climb on smooth vertical surfaces. Tiny 'hairs' on their toes work like a glue to make their feet sticky. They can even walk upside down along a ceiling or tree branch.

- **Geckos can see well** at night because their eyes are much more sensitive to light than ours.

▼ *This noisy gecko makes a loud 'to-kay' call which gives rise to its common name of 'tokay'. It lives in Southeast Asia, often near or in people's homes. Its large eyes help it see in the dark.*

- **Unlike other lizards**, geckos have impressive voices and they can make a range of sounds that they use to attract mates.

- **Geckos vary in size** from 2 cm to 30 cm. Most are less than 20 cm long.

- **Tokay geckos are some** of the largest geckoes and the noisiest. They hiss loudly when they are attacked and can deliver a nasty bite with their large jaws.

- **Leopard geckos** are boldly patterned with black spots on yellow, warty skin. They have fat tails to store food.

- **Geckos are usually** well-camouflaged and a good example of this is the northern leaf-tailed gecko. Its colouring and body shape allow it to blend into a background of leaves so it is almost invisible.

- **Kuhl's flying gecko** uses its webbed feet to glide as it leaps from a tree.

▶ *A Madagascar day gecko grows to 30 cm long. It has a stocky body and thick tail. It uses its sticky toe pads to cling to a tree, often perching upside down on the trunk.*

Skinks and their relatives

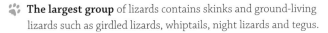

- **The largest group** of lizards contains skinks and ground-living lizards such as girdled lizards, whiptails, night lizards and tegus.

- **They mostly have long**, slender bodies and small legs.

- **Skinks are most common** in warm countries. They are difficult to see because they often scuttle around beneath leaf litter, or even burrow underground to hide.

- **Skinks that burrow** may have very small legs, or no legs at all.

- **Common lizards** live across large parts of Europe and Asia. Unusually, these lizards prefer cool climates and can survive within the Arctic Circle.

◄ Blue-tongued skinks are sometimes simply known as 'blue tongues' in their native Australia. A flash of a blue tongue can be enough to warn predators to stay away.

- **While some skinks** and their relatives lay eggs, others – such as the common lizard – give birth to live young.

- **Some members of this group** have very rough, tough scales that create an effective armour against predators.

- **Armadillo lizards have** armoured scales and roll themselves up into a coil when threatened.

- **Wall lizards**, such as the Ibiza wall lizard, are fast climbers that run across walls as they pursue insects.

- **Berber skinks have** orange markings on a blue-black body and can grow to 45 cm in length.

- **Major skinks live** in Australia and can grow to 70 cm long.

- **The eyed skink** has tiny limbs which it uses for digging and burrowing. It has a short tail that it loses when attacked.

DID YOU KNOW?
Some whiptail lizards can reproduce without a mate! This is called parthenogenesis.

Snakes

🐾 **Snakes are long**, thin reptiles with scaly bodies and no legs. There are about 3400 different species of snake, living all over the world, except Antarctica.

🐾 **The tiny thread snake** is only 11 cm in length but the giant reticulated python grows up to 10 m in length.

🐾 **All snakes are meat eaters**, and swallow prey whole.

🐾 **Egg-eating snakes** swallow eggs whole, then use the sharp, downward-pointing spines on their backbones to crack the shell. When the snake has swallowed the contents of the egg, it coughs up the shell.

🐾 **Some snakes kill** their prey by squeezing (constricting) it to death. Other snakes use poison.

▼ The colours and patterns on a royal python's skin are perfect for helping it hide in leaf litter on the ground of an open forest, or near fields. These snakes coil up into a ball shape if they are scared.

▲ *Most snakes, like the common krait, are shy and prefer to spend the day out of sight. At night, kraits become deadly predators with fast-acting venom. Humans can die within five hours of being bitten.*

About 700 snake species are poisonous. Snake poison is called venom and is injected into prey or predators using a snake's special teeth, called fangs.

About six times a year, snakes shed their outer layer of skin. This is called moulting, and it allows the snake to grow. A new, bigger skin grows under the old one.

Most snakes lay eggs in damp, warm places and leave them to hatch by themselves. A few female snakes, such as pythons, coil around their eggs to protect them from predators or bad weather while they develop.

A few snakes, such as boas, rattlesnakes, adders and most sea snakes, give birth to live young.

Sea snakes can dive to depths of 100 m to feed on fish. They have tails like oars to push them through water. The most poisonous snake in the world is the black-headed sea snake.

Pythons and boas

- **The six biggest snake** species in the world are all boas and pythons. These are the anaconda, boa constrictor, Indian python, reticulated python, African rock python and amethystine, or scrub python.

- **Pythons and boas** are constricting snakes. They wind their coils tightly around their victims until they die from suffocation or from shock.

- **Constrictors usually swallow** victims whole, then spend days digesting them. Their special jaws allow their mouths to open very wide. A large meal can be seen as a lump moving down the body.

▼ The green anaconda lies in water, waiting for its prey. It is big enough to kill a horse.

▲ *This snake has an iridescent sheen on its skin. Rainbow boas live in the humid jungles of Central and South America.*

- **Pythons live in Asia**, Indonesia and Africa. Boas and anacondas are the big constrictors of South America.

- **Boas lie in wait** for their victims. Like all snakes, they can go for weeks without food.

- **Tree boas are good climbers**. The emerald tree boa hangs from branches to seize birds in its teeth. It uses pits along its lips to sense the heat given off by its prey.

- **The markings** of boa constrictors give them excellent camouflage in a variety of habitats, from deserts to forests.

- **Boas have tiny remnants** of back legs, called spurs, which males use to tickle females during mating.

- **Anacondas spend time** in swampy ground or shallow water, lying in wait for their victims to approach for a drink. They are the heaviest snakes, weighing up to 227 kg.

- **Cuban wood snakes** are stocky constrictors that defend themselves by releasing a foul-stinking slime from their bottom.

215

Typical snakes

- **The largest family** of snakes is called the colubrid family, with about 2100 members.

- **They are also known** as typical snakes and they are found throughout the world except Antarctica – although most live in warm places.

- **Colubrids have large** plate-like scales on their heads. Their venomous fangs are at the back of their mouths. The two bones of their lower jaw are not connected.

- **Some members** of this group kill their prey by squeezing them to death, like constrictors. Others have up to three pairs of venomous fangs.

- **Boomslangs are deadly tree** snakes of Africa. They have large eyes and can accurately judge their distance from their prey – usually lizards and birds.

- **Common garter snakes** live far north and survive the winter by hibernating. Hundreds of them hibernate together and wake at the same time.

- **Corn snakes are a type** of rat snake and a vivid orange colour.

◄ Corn snakes are mostly nocturnal and live in parts of central and southeast United States.

🐾 **When a grass snake** is scared it produces a nasty-smelling liquid and plays dead – it lies upside down with its mouth open and tongue hanging out.

🐾 **A milk snake** is red, yellow and black – colours that often indicate danger. It is not venomous but looks similar to a coral snake, which does have deadly venom.

🐾 **A female** southern water snake can give birth to more than 50 young at a time.

Cobras and mambas

🐾 **Cobras and mambas** belong to a group of snakes called elapids. There are about 350 species of elapid and all of them are venomous.

🐾 **Unlike colubrids**, these snakes have fangs at the front of their mouths. This means they can quickly deliver a dose of venom.

🐾 **Coastal taipans** and copperheads are elapids that live in or around Australia. The coastal taipan is shy but it is still one of the most dangerous snakes because it moves fast and its venom is particularly powerful.

🐾 **Spitting cobras** spray venom at an attacker. They aim for the eyes and can fire with great accuracy.

🐾 **Black mambas** are dull and slender, making them difficult to spot. However, they are fast to attack and swift to move – slithering along the ground faster than a human can escape.

▶ The king cobra, or hamadryad, hunts other snakes to eat. It rarely comes into contact with humans, so does not pose a great threat to them. At a length of 3–5 m it is the world's longest venomous snake.

◀ The black mamba is especially dangerous – not just because of its speed but because it is active in the day and has very fast-acting venom.

- **Coral snakes** have red, black and yellow or white bands. There are about 40 species of coral snake and they live in the Americas.

- **Green mambas slither** through jungle trees with great speed, chasing their prey.

- **Sea kraits** live in the ocean. They have a flattened tail for swimming and even give birth at sea.

- **Some cobras warn** attackers to stay away by raising their heads and expanding their 'hoods'.

- **A cobra's hood** is made from its ribs, and it has the effect of making the reptile seem bigger and even more intimidating.

- **Indian cobras** are one of the most dangerous snakes in the world. They not only have deadly venom but they often live in fields, near rivers and alongside human homes.

- **King cobras are the only** snakes known to build nests. The female lays 20–40 eggs in her nest and guards them until they hatch.

Vipers

- **Vipers have long**, hinged fangs which they can move into the perfect position for striking and delivering venom. After use, the fangs are folded back up into the snake's mouth.

- **Vipers have broad heads** and rough scales that have ridges. Most of them have camouflaged skin and they hunt by lying in wait for prey to pass by before launching an attack.

- **There is only one** venomous snake in northwest Europe: the common adder. Like many other vipers, it is able to survive in a cold climate.

- **Gaboon vipers have wide,** triangular shaped heads and their thick, stocky bodies are camouflaged so they can move slowly through leaf litter. They hiss when they are scared.

▼ *The most dangerous snake in North America is the rattlesnake. It lives in grasslands, scrub and deserts and uses its rattle to warn other animals to keep their distance.*

▲ With its large, slow-moving body the African gaboon viper prefers to lie in wait for its prey to come close before striking. A female can give birth to as many as 30 youngsters at a time.

🐾 **A viper's venom kills** its victims by making their blood clot. Viper venom has been used to treat haemophiliacs (people whose blood does not clot well).

🐾 **Pit vipers of the Americas** hunt their warm-blooded victims using heat-sensitive pits on the side of their heads. They can track prey such as mice in total darkness.

🐾 **Most vipers** give birth to live young.

🐾 **Rattlesnakes are vipers** that live in warm, dry parts of southern USA and Mexico. They are fast hunters and quick to bite when surprised.

🐾 **The rattles of a rattlesnake** are made from layers of dead skin that collect around the animal's tail.

🐾 **Pit vipers that live** in trees wrap their tails around a branch so they can lunge their heads forwards to attack.

Turtles and tortoises

🐾 **Turtles and tortoises** are hard-shelled reptiles. With terrapins, they make up a group called the testudines, or chelonians.

🐾 **There are about** 300 species of testudines, living in warm places all over the world. They all lay their eggs on land, even those that live in rivers or the sea.

🐾 **The shield on the back** of a testudines is called a carapace. Its flat belly armour is called a plastron.

▼ *In general, turtles have flatter bodies than tortoises. This is a better shape for swimming. Green sea turtles use their large front legs like flippers to swim.*

◄ The high domed carapace of a tortoise is a strong structure that provides good defence against the strong jaws of a predator. Shovel-shaped front legs are used for digging.

🐾 **Most turtles and tortoises** have no teeth. Instead, their jaws have sharp edges for eating plants and tiny animals.

🐾 **North American** snapping turtles are the only testudines that can be dangerous to people.

🐾 **Giant tortoises** can weigh as much as three men, grow up to 1.3 m in length, and may live for over 200 years.

🐾 **The pancake tortoise's** flat shell allows it to squeeze under rocks to avoid predators and the hot sunlight in Africa.

🐾 **The giant leatherback** is the largest turtle, growing to 2 m in length. It is also the only soft-shelled sea turtle.

🐾 **Green turtles** swim about 2250 km from their feeding grounds off the coast of Brazil to their nesting beaches on Ascension Island in the south Atlantic Ocean.

DID YOU KNOW?
The tiny speckled padloper is the smallest tortoise in the world. It is just 6 cm long and hides from predators beneath rocks.

Galápagos tortoises

🐾 **The word** *galápago* means turtle in Spanish, and it was used to name the Galápagos Islands in the Pacific Ocean, where giant tortoises live.

🐾 **Galápagos tortoises** are the largest tortoises in the world, with a body length of up to 150 cm and a maximum weight of 320 kg.

▼ The long neck of a giant tortoise enables it to stretch and reach vegetation that other, smaller animals cannot reach. These tortoises' mouths are tough enough to munch through cacti plants.

🐾 **A giant tortoise** can live to be more than 100 years old.

🐾 **These giant reptiles** live on different islands. The tortoises on each island evolved with slight differences from those on neighbouring islands.

🐾 **In general**, tortoises that live on wetter islands have a more domed body than those on drier islands. Over time, they have adapted to their different environments and the food available – flatter shells allow tortoises on drier islands to reach plant matter that grows off the ground.

🐾 **Galápagos tortoises** are herbivores and spend most of the day grazing or resting in water.

🐾 **All giant tortoises** are listed as vulnerable, which means they may become extinct.

🐾 **Females dig** a nest in the ground and lay up to 16 eggs at a time. The eggs take about five months to hatch.

🐾 **Young tortoises** are in danger of being eaten by animals that humans have brought to the islands, such as rats.

🐾 **There is another type of** giant tortoise living on islands in the Indian Ocean. Aldabra giant tortoises can reach more than one metre in length and 250 kg in weight.

DID YOU KNOW?
Their slow metabolisms and large internal stores of water allow giant tortoises to survive for up to a year without eating or drinking.

225

Crocodilians

- **Crocodiles, alligators, caimans** and gharials are large reptiles that make up the group known as crocodilians. There are 13 species of crocodile, two alligators, six caimans and two gharials.

- **Crocodilian species** lived alongside the dinosaurs 200 million years ago.

- **Crocodilians are hunters** that eat a lot of fish, although larger species may eat animals as large as zebras.

- **A crocodilian's body** temperature is the same as its surroundings. They usually bask in the sunshine in the morning, then seek shade or go for a swim to cool off.

- **The biggest crocodilians** are saltwater crocodiles and Nile crocodiles, which can grow to 7 m in length.

- **Gharials have thin**, pointed snouts. They are named for the pot-shaped bump on males' snouts (*ghara* means 'pot' in Hindi). They are on the verge of extinction.

- **Crocodiles have thinner** snouts than alligators. One tooth on either side of their lower jaw is visible when their mouths are shut.

- **When her eggs hatch**, a mother Nile crocodile picks up her babies in her mouth and carries them to the water.

- **Alligators are found** both in the Florida Everglades in the USA and in the Yangtze River in China.

▼ Every year enormous herds of wildebeest travel through parts of Eastern Africa. Their ancient migration routes take them across rivers where hordes of hungry Nile crocodiles lie in wait.

DID YOU KNOW?

Crocodilians swallow objects such as pebbles to help their stomachs break down food.

Saltwater crocodiles

- **The saltwater crocodile** is the largest of all crocodilians and probably the biggest reptile alive today.

- **They can live in the sea** or freshwater areas. They are found around Australia, Southeast Asia and the western Pacific Ocean to Japan.

- **Few large, old crocodiles** are still alive because they have been the favourite targets of human hunters.

▼ *Despite its great size, a saltwater crocodile can easily haul its body out of the water. It can raise its body above its legs and even chase its prey on land.*

- **No one knows** for sure how long they may live, but it has been estimated that these crocodiles probably live to 70 years or more.

- **A special flap** at the back of a crocodile's mouth closes when the animal opens its mouth underwater.

- **Adults are strong enough** to grab prey from the water's edge. They attack large animals, such as wallabies and cows, but they also feed on other reptiles, fish and birds.

- **Although a crocodile** has a powerful bite it does not have much strength in the muscles that open its mouth – so it is almost impossible to stop a crocodile from biting, but it is quite easy to open its jaws.

- **Mothers take great care** of their young. They build a nest from plants and mud and lay about 50 eggs. They guard the eggs with great care while the baby crocodiles grow inside.

- **When the baby crocodiles** are ready to hatch they call their mother. She helps them to break out of their shells and carefully carries them to the water in her mouth.

- **Young crocodiles** stay with their mother for up to eight months. She protects them from predators, but few survive to become adults. They eat fish, insects and crabs.

- **Crocodiles are fast on land**, and superb swimmers. Saltwater crocodiles are particularly agile swimmers, and can twist and turn with speed.

Amphibians

What are amphibians?

- **Amphibians are animals** that live on land and in water. They can dry out very quicky so most of them spend all of their lives near water or in damp habitats.

- **They include frogs**, toads, newts and salamanders.

- **Amphibians have two** main life stages. The young are called tadpoles and when they change to become adults they go through a process called metamorphosis.

- **An amphibian** can't control its body temperature and is described as being cold-blooded.

- **The eggs of an amphibian** dry out very easily – because of this females usually lay their eggs in ponds, rivers, lakes or even in puddles.

- **Caecilians are legless** amphibians. They burrow underground and are rarely seen.

- **While some caecilians** lay eggs, others keep their eggs inside them until they hatch, giving birth to their young.

- **Amphibians have smooth**, moist skin and no scales. They have poison glands in their skin and many amphibians coat their bodies in foul-tasting, or toxic, substances.

- **When an amphibian is young**, and living in water, it uses gills to breathe. As an adult it can use simple lungs, or take in oxygen through its moist skin.

- **There are about 6640 species** of amphibian – many of them are endangered.

Many amphibian habitats have been destroyed or are currently threatened. They are also suffering from the effects of pollution and global climate change, which may have contributed to a fungal disease that is killing frogs in large numbers around the world.

▼ Barking frogs live in the southern United States. During the mating season, males attract females by sitting in treetops and producing loud vocalizations, which sound like dogs barking.

Newts and salamanders

▲ Male and female great crested newts look similar until mating time, when the crest on a male's back will grow bigger.

🐾 **Newts and salamanders** are amphibians with long, slender bodies. They all have four legs and a tail. Most of them live in Europe and Asia.

🐾 **In general**, salamanders spend their whole lives in water and newts spend most of their adult lives on land. Newts return to water to breed.

🐾 **The Californian newt** produces such deadly toxin that just one drop can kill thousands of mice.

🐾 **The largest salamanders** are the Japanese and Chinese giant salamanders. They can grow to more than one metre long. The smallest type lives in Mexico and measures less than 2 cm long.

- **Fire salamanders** have bright yellow patches on their black skin. This colouring warns predators to stay away – they make a nasty-tasting toxin in glands on their head.

- **Most amphibians** eat small invertebrates but there is one species of salamander – the Santa Cruz climbing salamander – that eats fungus too.

- **Olms are strange amphibians** that spend their whole lives in streams in caves. They prey on small invertebrates and they have feathery gills instead of lungs – even as adults.

- **Japanese giant salamanders** can live to the age of 50.

- **Axolotls are amphibians** that never metamorphose into an adult body form, but they are still able to breed. They live in just one lake in Mexico where they are protected to avoid extinction.

- **Sharp-ribbed salamanders** defend themselves using their ribs. These bones push through their skin and poison glands forming sharp, toxic points.

▼ Fire salamanders of Europe look similar to tiger salamanders of North America. This fire salamander's yellow poison glands can be seen on the side of its head.

Amphibian life cycles

- **Most amphibians** begin life as eggs that hatch to release tadpoles. The tadpoles must change into adults during a complex process called metamorphosis.

- **The word metamorphosis** means 'change of shape or form'.

- **A female amphibian** usually produces many eggs, called spawn. The spawn is released into water and is coated in a protective jelly.

- **The amount of time** it takes for an egg to hatch, and for a tadpole to grow into an adult, depends on the temperature. In warmer weather, these processes happen faster.

- **A female cane toad** can produce as many as 35,000 eggs when she spawns (lays her eggs).

- **Tadpoles are also called larvae** and the time that an amphibian spends as a tadpole is called the 'larval stage'.

- **A tadpole begins life** with feathery gills for breathing and a tail for swimming. As it grows it develops limbs and lungs, and its body becomes more like its adult form. It eventually loses its tail and begins to explore beyond the pond.

- **The tadpole of the paradoxical frog** is huge, reaching nearly 17 cm in length. The adult frog, however, is much smaller at less than 7 cm.

- **Male frogs and toads** croak to call females to them. Each species of frog or toad has its own special mating call. The mating call of a raucous toad sounds like a duck quacking.

- **Some female frogs** keep their eggs inside their body and give birth to baby frogs.

▼ *The way that an animal changes from egg to adulthood, and reproduces, is called its life cycle. Amphibians, such as this common frog have unusually complex life cycles.*

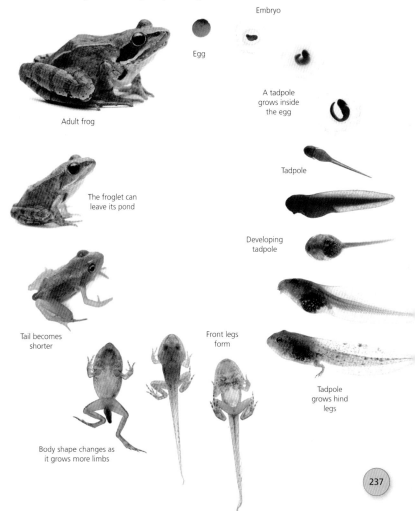

Embryo

Egg

Adult frog

A tadpole grows inside the egg

Tadpole

The froglet can leave its pond

Developing tadpole

Tail becomes shorter

Front legs form

Tadpole grows hind legs

Body shape changes as it grows more limbs

Toads

- **There are no major** differences between frogs and toads but, in general, toads crawl rather than hop and have a warty skin.

- **The common toad** is an adaptable creature. It is able to live in very high places – up to 8000 m in the Himalayas.

- **Male midwife toads** look after the eggs. To protect the young from predators the male winds them around his back legs and carries them until they are ready to hatch.

- **Common spadefoot toads** can live in dry places because they use their broad shovel-like feet to burrow into the ground and avoid drying-out.

- **The cane toad** originally came from the Americas but is now established in Australia. This is the world's largest toad and it eats almost any animal it can catch.

- **The cane toad produces venom** from glands behind its eyes. The venom is deadly to many animals.

- **Mexican burrowing frogs** spend most of their lives underground, only emerging after rain so they can breed.

- **Surinam horned frogs** are large – up to 20 cm – and equipped with strong jaws and teeth. They ambush their prey, such as mice and lizards, which they swallow whole.

- **When an oriental fire-bellied** toad is scared it raises its head and forelimbs to show off its red and black belly.

▶ A toad is at home in water or on land, as long as its skin does not dry out. Its long, strong legs and webbed feet enable it to swim, crawl or leap.

Frogs

🐾 **The world's smallest frogs**, including the Cuban frog and gold frog, are about one centimetre from nose to bottom. The biggest frog is the Goliath giant frog from West Africa. Its body measures about 30 cm long.

🐾 **A frog**, like a toad, catches its prey with a long sticky tongue that shoots out of its mouth.

🐾 **There are about 855 species** of tree frog. Most of them live in forests of the Americas and Australia. They have sticky toe pads that allow them to cling to upright surfaces, such as tree trunks.

🐾 **Glass frogs have green skin** on their backs, but the skin on their bellies is so thin it is transparent and the frogs' organs can be seen inside.

🐾 **The Java flying frog** leaps between trees and uses webs of skin between its toes to parachute gently down.

🐾 **Some tree frogs** lay their eggs underneath leaves that overhang streams and cover them with a thick froth to keep them moist. When the tadpoles hatch they drop into water below.

🐾 **Frogs have very long** hind limbs, which allow them to leap out of danger. Smaller frogs are usually better jumpers than big frogs.

🐾 **Dotted humming frogs** live with tarantula spiders, hiding in the spiders' burrows and eating ants that would otherwise feed on the spider's eggs.

🐾 **Frogs have four toes** on their front legs and five toes on their hind legs.

Gastric brooding frogs have strange life cycles. Females keep the tadpoles in their stomachs while they grow, and the froglets 'hatch' out of their mouths when they are developed. These frogs are so rare it is possible they are now extinct.

▼ The orange-thighed frog is an inhabitant of Australian rainforests. This tree frog spends most of its life in the treetops.

Poison arrow frog

- **Brightly coloured frogs** of Central and South American rainforests often have deadly toxins in their skin.

- **They are called poison arrow** frogs because rainforest people wipe poison from them on weapons before hunting. Poison arrow frogs are sometimes called poison dart frogs, or just poison frogs.

- **The Venezuela skunk frog** is one of the largest poison arrow frogs at 6.2 cm in length. It is also one of the smelliest because instead of producing a toxic skin secretion it makes a foul-smelling one instead. The smell is similar to that made by a skunk.

- **Poison arrow frogs** can make some poisons themselves, but they probably get most of their toxins from their diet of insects, such as ants.

- **They live** on the damp forest floor, among the leaf litter where they can find plenty of invertebrates to eat.

- **These amphibians are tiny**, but their bright colours ensure that predators can see them clearly – and are warned of their toxicity.

- **The golden poison arrow frog** is the most deadly discovered so far. Its poison is 20 times more dangerous than any other frog's poison.

- **Male blue poison frogs** look after the eggs once the female has laid them. He protects them for about 12 days until they hatch. Green and black poison dart frog fathers carry their tadpoles on their backs.

▶ *Male strawberry poison dart frogs battle over their territories, and often wrestle one another for the best habitats.*

DID YOU KNOW?

Some poison frog tadpoles eat frogspawn, or their brothers and sisters.

Fish

What are fish?

▲ *Great hammerhead sharks are large fish with a maximum length of 6 m. They live in warm shallow waters, especially near coral reefs.*

🐾 **Nearly 75 percent** of all fish live in the seas and oceans.

🐾 **Fish are mostly slim**, streamlined animals that live in water. Many are covered in tiny shiny plates called scales. Most have bony skeletons and a backbone.

🐾 **There are more than** 32,500 species of fish. They vary in size from the 8-mm-long pygmy goby to the 13-m-long whale shark.

- **There are three main groups** of fish, most of which are bony fish. A small group of about 1200 species, including sharks and rays, have skeletons made of cartilage. There are about 40 species of fish that do not have jaws, such as lampreys. These jawless fish have snake-like bodies and round, sucking mouths.

- **Fish are cold-blooded**. They breathe through gills – breathing organs that take oxygen from the water.

- **They have fins**, not limbs. Most have a pectoral fin behind each gill, two pelvic fins below to the rear, a dorsal fin on top of the body, an anal fin beneath, and a caudal (tail) fin.

- **Most bony fish** let gas in and out of their swim bladders so they can float at particular depths.

- **Some fish communicate** by making sounds with their swim bladder.

▼ *A blue marlin is a large bony fish that lives in the sea. Its tube-shaped body and large dorsal fin enables it to swim at top speeds of 80 km/h.*

247

Lungfish and coelacanths

- **Coelacanths and lungfish** belong to a group of fish called fleshy-finned fish. They use the large fins on their undersides to 'walk' along the sea bed.

- **Many millions of years ago**, relatives of fleshy-finned fish moved onto land and evolved into the ancestors of modern land-living vertebrates.

- **Lungfish breathe** using gills or lungs – they can breathe underwater and in air.

- **A lungfish gulps air** if its pool of water has little oxygen left in it. It can also use its fleshy fins to clamber out of its pool.

- **African lungfish survive** the dry season by burrowing into mud. They wrap mucus around their bodies to create a cocoon where they stay until the next rainy season.

- **Coelacanths are called** 'modern fossils' because they belong to a group of fish that were thought to have died out at the same time as the dinosaurs.

- **Coelacanths were first discovered** in 1938. There are two species: one lives in deep water near the coast of south-eastern Africa and the other lives near Sulawesi in Indonesia. Both types are endangered.

DID YOU KNOW?
A coelacanth has a big head but a tiny brain. The rest of the space is filled with fat.

🐾 **A coelacanth opens** its mouth wide to swallow large prey. It moves its fleshy fins like legs, one at a time, to move forwards on the sea bed.

🐾 **It is thought** that a coelacanth can live for 60 years, or longer. They grow to 2 m long.

▼ A coelacanth has an unusual middle lobe in its tail fin and a dark body that is covered in white flecks. Most coelacanths live alone, although some groups have been found living together in caves.

Coral reef fish

🐾 **Many colourful fish** species live in warm seas around coral reefs.

🐾 **Some butterfly fish** have a marking that resembles an eye near the tail to confuse predators, and can even swim backwards to complete the deception!

🐾 **Male triggerfish** can increase their colour to attract females.

🐾 **Cuckoo wrasse** are all born female, but big females change sex when they are between seven and 13 years old.

🐾 **Larger fish**, such as groupers, queue up for cleaner fish to go over them, nibbling away pests and dead skin. The banded coral shrimp cleans up pests in a similar way.

🐾 **The sabre-toothed blenny** looks similar to a cleaner fish. This allows it to swim up close to fish so that it can take a bite.

🐾 **The cheeklined Maori wrasse** changes colour to mimic harmless plant-eating fish, such as damselfish.

🐾 **Coral reefs are home** to many sea creatures. Large fish, such as sharks, visit this habitat to hunt, lay their eggs or give birth.

DID YOU KNOW?
Stonefish have 13 dorsal spines that deliver a dose of poison so deadly it can kill a person.

▶ *Clownfish live among a sea anemone's stinging tentacles because they provide a safe place to hide from predators. The clownfish are not affected by the anemone's stings.*

Coastal fish

- **At the coast** the sea is shallow and sunlight can reach the sea bed. Many ocean plants and seaweeds live here, making the coast an ideal habitat for fish.

- **Young fish often live** in coastal areas. They hide from predators among the plants and seaweeds.

- **Common stargazer fish** bury themselves in sand. Their eyes are on the top of their heads so they can see prey and predators above them. They have sharp venomous spines behind their gills, which they use to defend themselves.

- **Sand eels are long,** thin fish that live in sandy bays in northern Europe. They are preyed upon by puffins, which dive into the sea to catch them.

- **Wolf fish live in shallow water** and around deep sea corals in the North Atlantic Ocean. They have large teeth for cracking open shelled animals.

- **Capelin fish swim** to shallow water when it is time to lay their eggs. Each female lays up to 60,000 eggs in coastal sand.

▲ A puffin can hold up to 30 sand eels in its bill. These small fish bury themselves in the seabed and are very common in shallow European waters. Many marine animals feed on sand eels.

▲ *There are about 50 species of stargazer fish and they typically grow to about 75 cm long. They live in the Atlantic, Pacific and Indian Oceans and are most common in warm coastal waters.*

When it is time to mate, oyster toadfish make such loud grunting noises that they can be heard by people living nearby.

Unlike many fish, oysterfish are able to survive in the heavily polluted waters of some coastal areas.

East Atlantic red gurnards use the stiff spines on their fins to feel their way along the sea bed as they hunt for crustaceans, such as shrimps and crabs.

Some coastal fish, such as summer flounder, migrate between the sea and estuaries (where rivers meet the sea). They prefer to spend warmer months inshore, and migrate offshore for the winter and to spawn.

Open ocean fish

▲ *Many sharks live in the open ocean, including oceanic whitetips. This species has a huge range and is found in the three major oceans and the Mediterranean Sea.*

The biggest, fastest-swimming fish, such as swordfish and marlin, live near the surface of the open ocean, far from land. They often migrate vast distances to spawn (lay their eggs) or find food.

The swordfish can swim at up to 80 km/h. It uses its long spike to slash or stab squid.

The bluefin tuna can grow as long as 3 m and weigh more than 500 kg. It is also a very fast swimmer – one crossed the Atlantic in 60 days.

Barracudas are fearsome predators that hunt in packs. They have torpedo-shaped bodies to help them swim fast and sharp, dagger-like teeth to kill their prey.

Porcupine fish defend themselves by swallowing a lot of water so that their bodies inflate like balloons. Spines on the fish's skin then stick out, making it impossible for a predator to swallow such a prickly mouthful.

Fish that live in the open ocean must survive a range of temperatures and different levels of salinity (saltiness). They also have to cope with currents – undersea 'rivers' of flowing water.

Atlantic flying fish have large wing-like pectoral fins that they use to soar above the water. They leap out of the ocean to escape from the jaws of big predators, such as tuna.

Pilotfish swim alongside larger animals and feed on scraps of food that their companions leave behind.

▼ There are about 40 species of flying fish. They 'fly' by swimming extremely fast before leaping out of the water.

Deep-sea fish

- **Below 200 m** there is not enough light for plants to photosynthesise (make food using sunlight and oxygen).

- **At depth**, the water pressure is enormous and it is difficult for animals to survive.

- **Many deep-sea fish** are able to produce light on their bodies. This is called bioluminescence.

- **Deep-sea angler fish have** 'fishing rods' growing out of the top of their heads that glow in the dark. They feed on fish that are attracted to these glowing lights.

- **Pacific blackdragons have long**, snake-like bodies and enormous mouths lined with dagger-like teeth. They live at depths of up to 1000 m in the Eastern Pacific Ocean. Lights along their bodies lure little animals towards them.

- **There are about 250 species** of lanternfish. Males and females make different patterns of light so they can identify each other at mating time.

▶ *The strange structure dangling over the head of a viperfish is its lure, which attracts fish towards its mouth.*

- **Hatchetfish are so thin** they are very difficult to see except from the side. They have huge eyes so they can see even in dim light.

- **Sloane's viperfish hide** in the ocean depths during the day but they travel up towards the surface at night to feed.

- **The gulper eel lives** at depths of 2000–3000 m and has such a massive mouth it can swallow prey larger than itself.

- **A tripod fish** uses very long leg-like fins to 'walk' along the soft, squidgy mud on the floor of the deep sea. It keeps its mouth open so it can swallow any small animals that the currents bring its way.

- **Blobfish float above the sea bed** in deep waters around Australia and New Zealand. When they are taken out of water their bodies collapse like jelly.

▶ *Like many fish in this lightless habitat, deep-sea anglerfish have huge mouths and very long teeth. Males are tiny and attach themselves to the body of a female so they never need to search for a mate again.*

Freshwater fish

🐾 **Freshwater fish live** in rivers, lakes and ponds throughout the world. Some fish spend part of their lifecycle in fresh water and part of it in the sea.

🐾 **Although far more fish live** in the ocean, nearly half of all known species are found in fresh water.

▼ Red piranhas are about 30 cm long and are equipped with strong jaws and extremely sharp teeth that can slice through flesh. These fish live in rivers throughout much of South America.

🐾 **Elephantnose fish live in murky rivers** of West and Central Africa. They can sense electricity made by other animals' muscles and use this skill to find food and mates, and find their way around in dark water.

🐾 **An electric eel is not a true eel**, but a type of knifefish. It can make large amounts of electricity – enough to stun or even kill a human.

🐾 **The red-bellied piranha fish** has a reputation as a fearless predator that can hunt in a group and kill large animals. However, it mostly feeds on insects and small fish.

🐾 **Longnose gars grow** to 1.8 m long and hide among river plants so they can ambush other fish that come close.

🐾 **When an arapaima fish** cannot get enough oxygen it swims to the surface of a river and takes a big gulp of air through its mouth. These predators grow to 4 m long.

🐾 **Mexican tetras are small fish** that are either orange and live in rivers and creeks, or white and live in caves. Cave-dwelling tetras are blind.

🐾 **Tigerfish are fast-moving predators** that can swallow fish that are half their size.

🐾 **A freshwater butterfly fish** can leap out of a river to grab insects. Although one of these fish only measures about 10 cm it can leap up to one metre, using its large pectoral fins to glide over the water's surface.

Flatfish

- **There are over 700 species** of flatfish. They have no swim bladders, so can lie on the sea bed without floating.

- **All flatfish start life** as normal-shaped fish, but as they grow older, one eye slides around the head to join the other. The pattern of scales changes so that one side becomes the top and the other side becomes the bottom.

- **The upper side of a flatfish** is usually camouflaged to help it blend in with the sea floor.

- **Plaice lie on the sea bed** on their left side, while turbot lie on their right side.

- **The world's largest flatfish** is the halibut, which grows to over 2 m in length. Unlike other flatfish, it catches fish in open water instead of lying on the sea bed.

- **Peacock flounders** are decorated with blue rings, which are like the blue eyes on a peacock's feathers.

- **Most flatfish live in the sea**, but a few species can live in freshwater. The European flounder often migrates up rivers to find food.

DID YOU KNOW?
If they are placed on a board of black and white squares, some flatfish can change their colours to match the background.

- **The eggs of flatfish** contain oil droplets, which enable them to float at or near the surface of the sea.

- **Plaice feed mainly on worms** and other small sea creatures, using their sensitive skin to find their food mainly by touch.

▲ Both of this peacock flounder's eyes are on one side of its head. This fish is commonly found in coral reefs of the Atlantic Ocean and it can change its colour to suit its surroundings.

Cod, anglerfish and relatives

Most of the members of this large fish family live near the sea bed, although some form large shoals that swim in the open ocean.

Cod, hake, pollock and haddock are all fished in vast amounts for humans to eat.

Atlantic cod are predators with long slender bodies. They can grow large – up to 90 kg – but such big specimens are extremely rare now as this species has been over-fished.

Anglerfish have broad, flattened bodies that are camouflaged so they blend into the sea bed.

▼ *An Atlantic cod has a long, strong body and a pointed snout. These fish swim towards the coast when it is time for them to lay their eggs. One female can lay several million eggs at a time.*

◄ *Incredible camouflage helps sargassumfish, a type of anglerfish, to hide from predators that include their relatives – these fish often turn cannibal and eat their own kind.*

🐾 **A fleshy growth** on an anglerfish's dorsal fin works like a fishing rod with bait to tempt other fish to come close. The anglerfish then opens its huge mouth and sucks its prey in.

🐾 **The Antarctic cod manages** to survive in the freezing oceans around the Antarctic by having a chemical antifreeze in its blood.

🐾 **Roughbar frogfish** are a type of anglerfish that look like rocks covered in seaweed.

🐾 **A female Alaskan Pollock** can produce up to 15 million eggs in just one year.

🐾 **Burbots live in cold**, dark rivers and lakes around the North Pole. They survive under layers of ice and hunt any small animal – such as insect larvae – that they find.

🐾 **Northern cavefish** are freshwater members of the family. They are small, pink and blind.

🐾 **Ventfish live in the ocean** around the Galápagos Islands, where hot steam and water pours out of the sea bed. They eat bacteria that thrive at these deep-sea vents.

Catfish and relatives

- **Catfish and their close relatives** belong to a group of freshwater fish with about 8000 members. They have a special set of bones that connect to their ears and give them excellent hearing.

- **The large catfish family** is divided into four groups: milkfish and their relatives, cyprinids, characins and catfish.

- **There are about 2900 species** of catfish. They have long, fleshy threads of skin, called barbels, around their jaws. A catfish uses them to feel its way along a river bed, finding food to eat.

- **Wels catfish grows** to 4.5 m long and is among the largest freshwater fish in the world. It is a slow-moving predator that can attack big animals such as birds.

- **An electric catfish produces** an electrical charge of up to 400 volts. It uses this skill to stun prey, or to keep predators at a safe distance.

- **Cyprinids do not have teeth** but can grind their food using hard areas in their mouths. Carps, minnows and goldfish are cyprinids.

- **Characins are similar to cyprinids** but they have a small fin – the adipose fin – in front of the tail.

- **Most characins are found** in South America. They eat a range of food including plants, small invertebrates and other fish. Piranhas and tetras are characins.

- **Bitterlings are a group** of fish that lay their eggs inside a freshwater mussel. When the baby fish hatch they stay inside the mussel for up to a month while they grow.

DID YOU KNOW?

Splash tetras leap out of the water and lay their eggs on overhanging leaves. This prevents the eggs being eaten by predators.

▲ The wels catfish lives in European rivers, prowling the muddy bottoms where it hunts shelled animals and fish. It is rarely seen because it is usually active at night.

Herrings and relatives

- **This family includes herrings**, shads, pilchards and anchovies. They normally feed on small animals that float in the ocean.

- **Herrings and their relatives** often swim in vast shoals of tens of thousands of fish, and are caught in large numbers by the fishing industry.

▼ *The largest shoals of herring gather in the breeding season when the water is warm. The shoals attract fast-swimming predators such as sailfish.*

- **As they swim**, they keep their mouths open and filter out their prey using gill rakers – specially adapted gills that work like sieves to catch food and let water pass through.

- **Anchovies are small** – up to 25 cm – slender fish with silvery scales. They are found in all of the world's oceans.

- **Shoals of California pilchards** used to contain millions of fish. Their numbers plummeted after many years of over-fishing and they nearly died out in the 1950s. Pilchards are also known as sardines.

- **Atlantic herring spend** daylight hours in deep water but swim to the surface as night falls to feed near the surface.

- **American shad live in the ocean**, but swim into rivers at breeding time. They lay their eggs in fresh water and a female can lay 600,000 eggs at a time.

- **Herrings and their relatives** are more common in the northern hemisphere than south of the Equator. They mostly feed near the coasts, although some species do live in the open ocean.

- **The largest member** of the family is the blackfin wolf-herring. It grows to one metre long and has two long, fang-like teeth.

- **Some members of this family** travel far in search of food and cover thousands of kilometres in a single journey that can take several years.

Eels

- **Eels are long**, slimy fish that look like snakes. Most eels do not have scales and there are about 800 species living all over the world. Baby eels are called elvers.

- **True eels all develop** from leaf-shaped larvae that drift on the ocean surface. Some species migrate back to rivers to breed.

- **Migrating eels are thought** to find their way partly by detecting weak electric currents created by the movement of the water.

- **When European eels hatch** in the Sargasso Sea they are carried northeast by the ocean current, developing as they go into tiny transparent eels called glass eels.

- **Moray eels are huge** and live in tropical waters, hunting fish, squid and cuttlefish.

- **Avocet snipe eels have** slender bodies and whip-like tails. They live in deep water and their long, beak-like jaws are lined with teeth. When males become adult they lose all their teeth.

- **Electric eels** are not true eels. They can produce an electric shock of 500 volts.

- **Garden eels live in colonies** on the sea bed, poking out from holes in the sand to catch food drifting by. Their colonies look like gardens of strange plants.

DID YOU KNOW?

Every autumn, some European common eels migrate over 7000 km, from the Baltic Sea in Europe to the Sargasso Sea near the West Indies, to lay their eggs.

▶ The skin of a yellowmouth moray eel is coated with a toxic slime that probably deters predators and keeps the animal free from parasites.

Migration

- **Long animal journeys** are called migrations.

- **Many species of fish** go on migrations to find food or mates, or to lay their eggs in a safe place.

- **Although some fish** always migrate to the same location no one knows how they find their way. Sometimes they are carried on their migrations by ocean currents.

- **Some migrations** are not across oceans, but up or down through the water – this is called a vertical migration.

- **Fish that migrate vertically** often spend the day in dark, deep water where they can hide from predators. They swim to the upper levels of the ocean at night to feed.

- **Most sharks** live in seas and oceans, but some bull sharks spend most of their lives in lakes and rivers – they migrate to and from the ocean.

- **Bluefin tuna prefer** to hunt in warm water so they migrate across the oceans to avoid being in cold water during the winter months.

- **Salmon are ocean fish** but they migrate to rivers to spawn. Sockeye salmon are blue-black but when they leave the ocean their bodies turn red and their heads turn green.

- **Eels are migrating fish** that can live in both salty ocean water and fresh water. Adults can even wriggle across damp ground.

- **Pikeminnows are freshwater fish** of the Colorado River. They make migrations of up to 200 km at spawning time. They grow to around one metre long, although there are records of pikeminnows with a length of nearly 2 m.

▼ *Atlantic bluefin tuna migrate between the places where they feed and the places where they lay their eggs. Their journeys can take them across the Atlantic, and a distance of 6000 km.*

Salmon

- **Salmon are river and sea fish** caught or farmed in huge quantities for food.

- **All salmon are born** in rivers and lakes far inland. They then swim down river and out to sea.

▼ *Fish such as the sockeye salmon – that migrate up a river to lay their eggs – are described as anadromous. Sockeye salmon spend most of their lives in the North Pacific Ocean and cold surrounding seas.*

- **Adult salmon spend anything** from six months to seven years in the oceans, before returning to rivers and swimming upstream to spawn (lay their eggs).

- **Spawning salmon return** to the stream they were born in, up to 3000 km inland. They may find their home stream by sensing the chemical and mineral content of the water.

- **Some salmon species**, including the chinook, spawn in North American rivers running into the North Pacific. Males fight each other to win a female and her nest.

- **Cherry salmon spawn** in eastern Asian rivers, and amago salmon spawn in Japanese rivers.

- **The female salmon scrapes** a nest called a redd in the gravel on the river bed. She lays between 8000 and 17,000 eggs in her redd.

- **When salmon first hatch**, they are called alevins or fry. At first they feed on a yolk sac attached to their body. When the yolk runs out, they start to feed on insect larvae and small invertebrates.

- **When young salmon** are a few centimetres in length, they develop dark blotches on their body for camouflage and are called parr. When the salmon head for the sea, the marks become covered by a silvery pigment and the fish are then called smolt.

- **Young salmon spend** between one and five years in the freshwater of rivers before they head for the sea.

Spiny-rayed fish

- **The largest group of fish** contains more than 13,000 species. They are spiny-rayed fish – which means they have tough spines in or near their dorsal fins.

- **The smallest spiny-rayed fish** are less than one centimetre long but the largest grow to 8 m.

- **There is a huge variety of shape**, colour and lifestyle in this group, and they are found in most of the world's watery habitats.

- **Stickleback fathers** look after the nest and eggs, fanning the water above them to bring oxygen to the growing fry (baby fish).

- **Guppies give birth** to live young. There are about 300 species of guppy and they live in fresh water around the Caribbean and northern South America.

- **Despite its name**, the largescale foureyes fish has two eyes. They are raised high on the fish's head, and allow it to see above and below water at the same time when swimming along the surface.

- **Oarfish have been rarely seen**, so little is known about their lifestyles. They have snake-like bodies that can reach 8 m long and the spiny rays on their heads make a crest.

DID YOU KNOW?
The John Dory fish has huge spines on its back and it extends its jaws to grab hold of prey that swims past.

- **Stonefish have venomous spines** and they are one of the deadliest fish in the world.

- **They lie still** on the sea bed, especially around coral reefs, and are so perfectly camouflaged that they are almost impossible to see.

Emperor angelfish are boldly coloured and patterned, but the young fish often look different to their parents. They make a loud sound when they are scared.

▼ *Like many other coral fish, the emperor angelfish has bold patterns and bright colours. Adults often look very different to the young fish.*

Seahorses and pipefish

🐾 **Most seahorses and their relatives** – pipefish, flute mouths, shrimp fish and snipe fish – live in the sea.

🐾 **Seahorses and their relatives** are a type of spiny-rayed fish.

▼ *Seahorses and leafy sea dragons are poor swimmers so they rarely move far. They cling on to seaweed to stop themselves being carried away by water currents.*

- **Seahorses have heads** that resemble horses and gripping tails like monkeys, to hold onto corals and plants.

- **The small, transparent fin** on its back pushes the sea horse through the water, beating as fast as 20 or 35 times a second. It steers with fins on the sides of its head.

- **Seahorses suck up shrimps** in their long hollow jaws. A young seahorse can eat 3500 shrimps a day.

- **They have armoured** outer skeletons that support and protect their internal organs. They do not have ribs, but they do have a bony internal skeleton.

- **A female seahorse** lays her eggs in a pouch on the front of the male's body. The male carries the eggs until the young emerge through a hole in the top of the pouch.

- **Leafy sea dragons are closely** related to seahorses. Their bodies are covered in leaf-like flaps, which camouflage them against the seaweeds.

- **A seahorse can change colour** to match its habitat and keep out of sight of predators.

- **The pipefish** has a long, straight body, with tiny fins and the same sort of body armour as a sea horse. Most pipefish swim horizontally, but some swim vertically.

- **Like seahorses**, male pipefish carry the eggs until they hatch.

Skates and rays

- **Skates and rays belong** to a group of over 650 species of fish. It includes stingrays, electric rays, manta rays, eagle rays, sawfish and guitarfish.

- **Most skates and rays** have flat, almost diamond-shaped bodies, with pectoral fins elongated into broad wings. Guitar fish and sawfish have longer, more shark-like bodies.

- **The gills and mouths** of skates and rays are on the undersides of their bodies.

- **They have no bones**. Like sharks, they are cartilaginous fish – their skeleton is made of rubbery cartilage instead.

- **Skates and rays live** mostly on the ocean floor, feeding on shellfish.

- **Manta rays live near** the surface and feed on plankton.

- **Stingrays get their name** from their whip-like tail with its poisonous barbs.

▶ Stingrays use their poisonous barbs for defence. The blue-spotted stingray lies on the sea bed but can whip its tail over its body to plunge its toxin into an attacker.

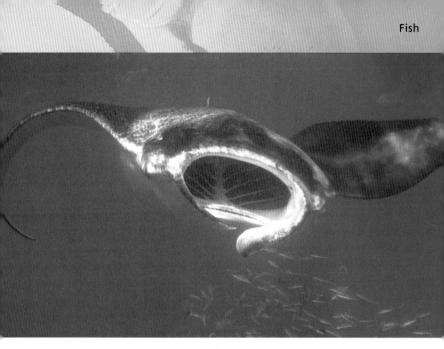

▲ *As a manta ray swims it constantly funnels water into its mouth, bringing food into the cavernous opening. Food is trapped there and swallowed. The water is passed out of the fish's gills.*

- **The Atlantic manta ray** is the biggest ray, often more than 7 m wide and 6 m in length.

- **Electric rays are tropical rays** that are able to give off a powerful electric charge to defend themselves against attackers.

DID YOU KNOW?
The black torpedo ray can give a 220 volt shock – as much as a household electric socket.

279

Slow-moving sharks

- **All sharks are closely** related to skates and rays, and have skeletons made of bone-like cartilage.

- **While many fast sharks** have torpedo-shaped bodies, others are slow movers that stay near the sea bed.

- **Carpet sharks** often have highly patterned skin and flattened bodies. There are many types, but they commonly swim near the sea floor as they look for animals, such as crabs, to eat.

- **Sharks either lay eggs** or give birth to live young. Shark eggs are protected by rubbery cases called mermaid's purses.

- **Spotted wobbegongs** are carpet sharks that are so well camouflaged they can lie in wait for an unsuspecting animal to come close – and then launch an attack.

- **Bamboo sharks** have strong fins that they can use to 'walk' on the sea bed or clamber along rocks and coral reefs.

- **A sawshark's long saw-shaped** snout is lined with sharp teeth. As the sawshark cruises along the sea bed it uses its saw to swipe through the sand and feel for prey.

- **Sharks don't have scales**. Instead they have denticles, which are made of enamel (like teeth) and are rough to the touch.

- **Whale sharks** do not hunt large animals. They use their gills to collect plankton (small animals and plants that float in the sea).

▶ *Whale sharks are most commonly seen in warm coastal waters, especially around coral reefs. They can make incredible migrations and one individual was found to have swum 13,000 km in just over three years.*

DID YOU KNOW?

The largest carpet sharks – and the largest fish in the world – are whale sharks, which swim slowly at the sea's surface. A whale shark can grow to 12 m or more.

Fast-moving sharks

- **Most sharks are active**, agile swimmers that race through the oceans when they are pursuing their prey – usually other fish, turtles and mammals such as seals.

- **A young shark** is called a pup.

- **Most sharks** have good eyesight and an incredible sense of smell and taste. They can detect the electrical fields given off by other animals.

- **The fastest shark** is believed to be the shortfin mako, which can reach top speeds of 80 km/h or more.

- **Hammerheads** have a bizarre appearance. Their hammer-shaped heads help them to locate their prey more easily and to change direction quickly.

- **The tail of a thresher shark** is almost as long as its body. It uses its huge tail to thrash and wallop its prey, stunning it so it is easier to catch and eat.

- **A fast shark's main weapons** are its large, sharp teeth.

- **Although shark teeth** are easily broken and lost there are many rows of teeth growing at a time, and new ones constantly move forwards to replace them.

- **Tiger sharks** are sometimes called 'bins with fins' because they bite and swallow almost anything they can find.

- **The bendy skeleton** and powerful muscles of a fast shark allow it to move its body from side to side as it swims, propelling it through the water when it needs a burst of speed.

▲ *Most fast-moving sharks look similar. The faint stripes on a tiger shark's flanks help to distinguish it from other species. The size and shape of teeth, snout, fins and tails are also used to identify fast sharks.*

A shark's sharp senses can detect one part of blood in one million parts of water.

Most fast sharks must keep swimming at all times, or sink. Whitetip reef sharks are able to rest on the seafloor by pumping water across their gills.

Great white shark

- **The most famous** of all sharks is the great white, also known as a white pointer. It can grow up to 6 m long.

- **Great white sharks** live in warm and cold waters of all oceans.

▼ Like many other sharks, great whites are at some risk of extinction because humans hunt them. This is a species of shark that does not thrive in captivity but tourists are often given the opportunity to observe them in the wild.

DID YOU KNOW?

The bite of a great white is about three times stronger than that of a lion.

🐾 **A great white has a massive mouth** that is filled with very sharp, triangular teeth arranged in several rows. There are 25–30 teeth in each row.

🐾 **They are able to keep** their bodies warmer than their surroundings. This means they can swim fast even in cold water.

🐾 **A great white** can lift its head out of water to look around before it attacks. It is thought that great whites may be able to see colour.

🐾 **Males and females** gather at mating places during spring and summer. Females carry up to 14 pups in their body, giving birth about 12 months after mating.

🐾 **A newborn great white** is about 1.2 m long.

🐾 **Some great whites** go on long migrations. One shark travelled nearly 11,000 km in just 99 days.

🐾 **Like many fast sharks**, great whites save energy by cruising through the ocean slowly. They only speed up when they are chasing prey.

🐾 **After taking a huge bite** of its prey, the great white often withdraws and then attacks again.

🐾 **It shakes its head** from side to side while biting hard to do maximum damage to its victim.

🐾 **Great whites eat** a variety of animals including fish, squid, crabs, seabirds and turtles. They also eat mammals such as seals, dolphins and porpoises.

Invertebrates

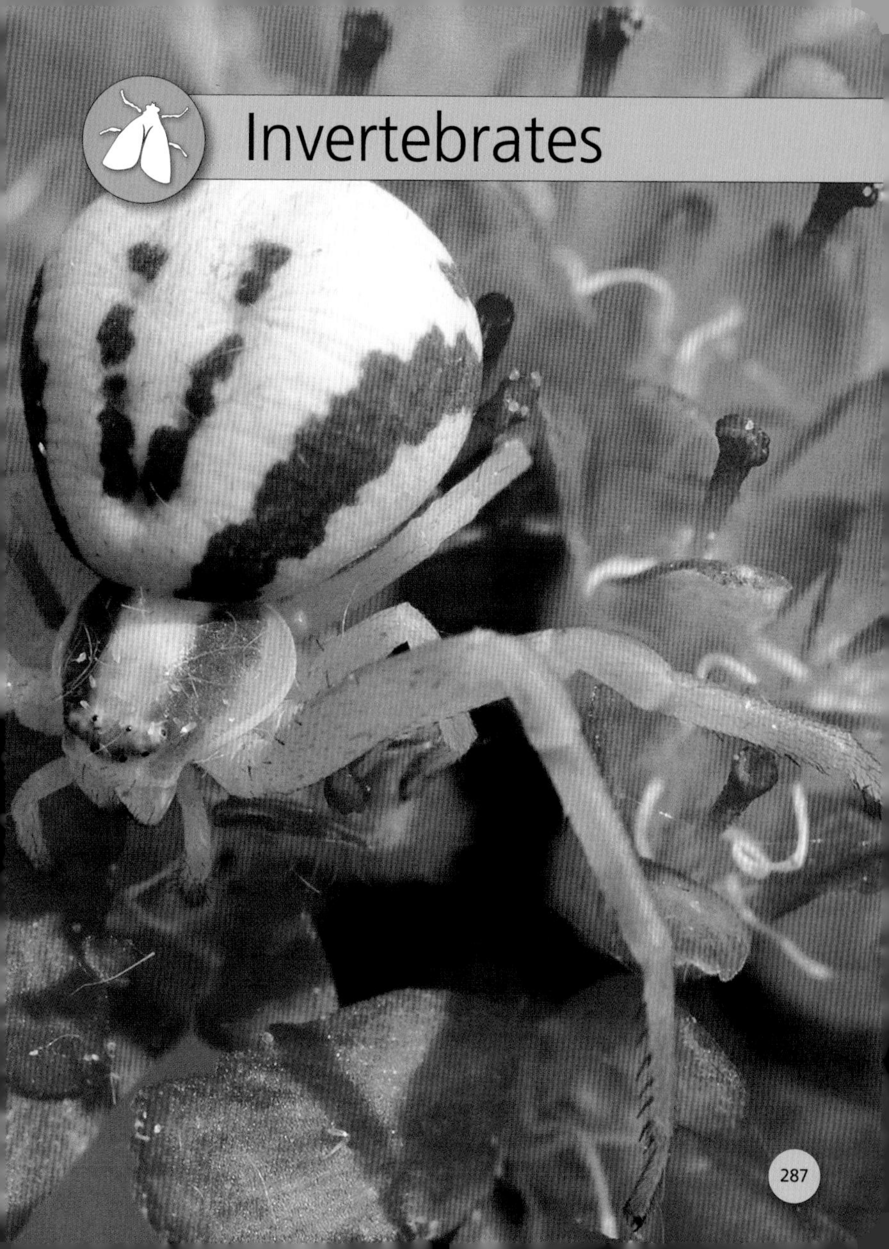

What are invertebrates?

- **Invertebrates are animals** without backbones or any other bones inside their bodies. They are cold-blooded and include insects, spiders, crabs, jellyfish and squid.

- **At least 99 percent** of all animal species are invertebrates. They are divided into over 30 groups, and probably include over five million species.

▼ The nautilus belongs to a group of invertebrates called molluscs. Its shell is mostly full of gas, which makes it buoyant. The animal controls its buoyancy so it can move up and down in the ocean water.

▶ *A ladybird is a beetle – one of the most varied groups of insects. Most ladybirds feed on garden pests.*

- **Invertebrates are usually** smaller than vertebrates (animals with backbones). Some forms are microscopic.

- **The biggest invertebrates** are the 16-m-long giant squid and the even larger colossal squid.

- **In 2007**, scientists discovered a claw from a giant sea scorpion, which lived between 460 and 255 million years ago. This giant invertebrate was 2.5 m in length.

- **The bodies** of some invertebrates are supported by an external skeleton. This skeleton cannot grow so it has to be shed (moulted) to allow the invertebrate to grow.

- **There are at least** one million different kinds of insects, and they are common all over the world.

- **Insects have six legs** and a body divided into three parts – the head, thorax and abdomen.

- **Insects do not have lungs**. Instead, they breathe through holes in their sides called spiracles, linked to their body through tubes called tracheae.

Worms

Worms are long, slender invertebrates with soft bodies. There are three main types of worm: flatworms, roundworms and segmented worms.

Many flatworms are parasites that live inside other animals' bodies. Parasites damage or kill their hosts (the animals that they live in, or on).

Tapeworms can grow to up to 30 m long, which makes them some of the longest animals on the planet.

A tapeworm lives inside an animal's intestines and absorbs food directly into its body.

A fluke is a worm that can live in up to four different hosts. The liver fluke spends part of its life inside a freshwater snail and part of it inside a human liver.

There are about 20,000 different types of roundworm and most of them are tiny. They can live in water, on land and inside animals or plants. They are also known as nematode worms.

▶ Earthworms are most active at night, when there are fewer predators around. They are an important source of food for many vertebrates.

▲ *Christmas tree worms attach themselves to the sea floor and create a home for other animals, such as small fish, which hide among them.*

Earthworms are a very common type of segmented worm. Each body part or 'segment' contains a set of organs.

As an earthworm burrows through soil it moves nutrients and air through the ground, which helps plants to grow.

Most segmented worms live in the sea. They are called bristleworms.

Many bristleworms build a protective tube around their body. Their feeding tentacles reach out beyond the tube and catch tiny particles of food that float past.

Leeches are blood-sucking segmented worms. When a leech bites into its host it injects substances that stop the blood from clotting so it can drink lots of blood in one go.

When a leech feeds on blood its body can swell up to ten times its normal size.

Corals and anemones

- **Sea anemones are tiny**, meat-eating animals that look a bit like flowers. They cling to rocks and catch tiny prey with their tentacles.

- **Coral reefs** are made from billions of tiny, sea-anemone-like animals called coral polyps and their skeletons.

- **They are the undersea** equivalent of rainforests, teeming with fish and other sea life.

- **Coral polyps** live all their lives in just one place, either fixed to a rock or to dead polyps.

▼ A sea anemone's tentacles are covered in tiny stinging cells called nematocysts. They use them to kill or stun their prey.

▶ Healthy corals create a natural, colourful habitat. However, coral is easily damaged and the polyps are very sensitive to environmental change. Dead coral turns white and is described as 'bleached'.

- **When coral polyps die**, their stony skeletons build up one on top of the other to become a coral reef.

- **Coral reefs only form** in clean, warm, salty water that is shallow enough to allow sunlight to reach the corals.

- **Fringing reefs stretch** from the seashore, while barrier reefs form long underwater walls a little way offshore.

- **The Great Barrier Reef** off northeastern Australia is the longest reef in the world, stretching for nearly 2000 km. It can be seen from space (up to 200 km up) and is the only non-human, animal activity visible from space.

- **Coral atolls** are ring-shaped islands that formed from fringing reefs around old volcanoes (which have long since sunk beneath the waves).

- **Coral reefs take thousands** or millions of years to form. The Great Barrier Reef started to grow about two million years ago but individual periods of coral reef growth have probably lasted for between 5000 and 15,000 years.

Jellyfish

- **Jellyfish are sea creatures** with bell-shaped, jelly-like bodies, and long stinging tentacles.

- **Biologists call an adult jellyfish** a medusa, after the mythical Greek goddess Medusa, who had wriggling snakes for hair.

- **They belong to a large** group of sea creatures called cnidarians, which also includes corals and anemones.

- **A jellyfish moves by** squeezing water from beneath their body. When a jellyfish stops squeezing, it slowly sinks.

- **Their tentacles are** covered with stinging cells called nematocysts, used to catch prey and for protection. The cells explode on contact, driving poisonous threads into the victim.

- **Jellyfish vary in size** from a few millimetres to over 2 m.

- **The bell of one giant jellyfish** measured 2.29 m across. Its tentacles were over 36 m long.

- **The Portuguese man-of-war** is not a true jellyfish. It is a living collection of polyps and medusae. One polyp forms a gas-filled float, while others catch and digest food.

- **The long tentacles** of the lion's mane jellyfish stretch out behind its body for up to 30 m. Stinging cells on the tentacles paralyze fish, plankton or other jellyfish while the lion's mane jellyfish feeds.

DID YOU KNOW?
The poison of the Australian box jellyfish can kill a human in less than five minutes.

▲ Jellyfish have little control over their direction of movement and largely rely on water currents to bring prey towards their tentacles.

Starfish and sea urchins

- **Starfish are not fish**, but belong to a group of sea creatures called echinoderms, meaning 'spiny skinned'.

- **Sea urchins and sea cucumbers** are also echinoderms.

- **Starfish have star-shaped bodies**. They feed mostly on shellfish, prising them open with their arms. The starfish inserts its stomach into its victim and sucks out its flesh.

▼ *Starfish are extraordinary animals with no brains or blood. They are believed to live very long lives because they can keep regenerating.*

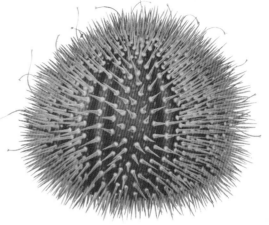

▶ The hard skin of a sea urchin is called a test. When the animal dies a thin outer skin and spines fall away, leaving just the tough test, which may wash up on the beach.

- **Starfish have** up to 2000 tube feet, which are like small balloons full of seawater. They are used for moving, as well as to take in food and oxygen from the seawater.

- **If a starfish sheds** one of its arms to escape a predator, or if one of its arms is crushed or bitten off, a new arm grows to take its place. This is called regeneration.

- **Sea urchins** are ball-shaped creatures. Their shell is covered with bristling spines, which can be poisonous.

- **A sea urchin's spines** are used for protection. Urchins also have sucker-like feet for moving.

- **Their mouths are just holes** with five teeth, located on the underside of the sea urchins' bodies.

- **Sea cucumbers have leathery skin** and a covering of chalky plates called spicules.

- **When threatened**, a sea cucumber expels pieces of its gut as a decoy and swims away. It grows a new one later.

297

Molluscs

- **Molluscs are a huge and varied group** of animals, but most of them live in the seas and oceans.

- **Shellfish, octopuses, snails** and squid are all types of mollusc.

- **Although some molluscs** are as small as a fingernail others can grow enormous – such as the colossal squid.

- **Marine molluscs** can grow large because the salty water supports their great weight.

- **Most molluscs have** a well-developed head. One mollusc group – the cephalopods – contains the most advanced and intelligent species.

- **A large part of a mollusc's body** is usually taken up with a 'foot'. This is a muscular body part that is used in movement.

- **The surface** of a mollusc's body is called a mantle. The mantle includes the shell, if there is one.

- **The shell of shelled molluscs** such as mussels and snails is made of calcium carbonate, a white chalky substance that is common in many rocks.

- **A mollusc's mouth** often contains a rough ribbon-like tongue that is covered with tiny 'teeth'. It is called a radula and it is used to scrape at food.

▶ Cuttlefish are related to squid and octopuses and have an incredible ability to change colour. There are more than 100 species of cuttlefish.

- **Marine molluscs** breathe using gills that grow in a space beneath their mantle.

- **Chitons are small marine molluscs** that have shells made of eight plates. They are oval in shape and live on the seabed where they graze on plants.

- **Tusk shells** are long, slender shelled animals that burrow into the sand. Little tentacles on their heads grab food that floats by.

Land slugs and snails

▲ The shell of a giant African land snail can measure up to 20 cm long. These molluscs feed on plant matter and live in warm, damp places. They are most active at night.

Eighty percent of all molluscs belong to a group called the gastropods, including slugs and snails. Although most gastropods live in the sea, many also live on land, where they mostly feed on plants.

- **Snails have shells**, but slugs do not. Snails that live on land have thinner shells than those that live in the water.

- **Land-living gastropods** are more common in wet, damp or cool places because they can dry out very easily. Snails and slugs breathe through their skin, which must be damp in order for the gases to pass through.

- **A thick layer of slime**, or mucus, helps a slug or snail to keep its body moist. It also helps the animal to slither over hard ground.

- **Snail slime is so thick** that it can protect an animal as it crawls over sharp, jagged edges.

- **Slugs and snails** cannot move fast, so they rely on their burrowing and hiding skills to stay safe from predators, such as birds and foxes.

- **Freshwater snails** live in ponds and rivers. Some of them breathe with gills but others breathe air.

- **The great grey slugs** of western Europe court by circling each other for over an hour on a branch, then launching themselves into the air to hang together from a long trail of mucus.

▶ The red triangle slug is the largest native Australian slug, growing to 14 cm long. Unlike most European slugs it has just one set of tentacles. It grazes on small plants growing on tree bark.

Octopuses and squid

- **Octopuses, squid, cuttlefish and nautiluses** belong to a family of molluscs called cephalopods, which all live in the sea.

- **Octopuses and squid** seize their prey, such as fish, with long arms that are covered in strong suckers.

- **The most intelligent invertebrates**, octopuses and squid have both long- and short-term memories. They can remember solutions to problems, and then go on to solve similar problems.

- **All octopuses** have two very large eyes, and a beak-like mouth.

- **When threatened**, squid and octopuses produce a cloud of black or brown ink to confuse predators.

▶ Octopuses live in salt water but they are able to clamber on to land and travel short distances. They have three hearts and blue blood.

- **Squid have an internal shell**, called a pen, in the middle of their bodies. Cuttlefish also have an internal shell – the cuttlebone.

- **The smallest octopus** is 2.5 cm across. The biggest measures 6 m from tentacle tip to tentacle tip.

- **A squid has eight arms** and two tentacles and swims by forcing a jet of water out of its body.

- **Nautiluses are the only cephalopods** with external shells. They can have as many as 90 arms but no suckers. Animals that looked similar to today's nautiluses swam in the world's oceans 500 million years ago.

Giant Pacific octopuses

- **The giant Pacific octopus** lives throughout the Pacific, especially near the coast and on the sea bed. It is the world's largest octopus species, and it can grow up to 3 m long.

- **These secretive animals** spend much of their time lurking in rocky crevices or beneath boulders, in dens.

- **They have no shells**, so their bodies are soft and can be squashed into small places.

- **Like other octopuses**, this cephalopod is a master of disguise and can change the colour of its skin to blend in with its surroundings. Its normal colour is reddish-brown.

- **A giant Pacific octopus** has a large brain, two eyes and eight arms that are covered with suckers. Each arm has suckers that are used to grab prey such as fish and other molluscs.

- **The arms and suckers** are also used to sense the octopus's surroundings. They are sensitive to touch and to chemicals in the water.

- **All octopuses have short lives**, and the giant Pacific octopus rarely lives beyond the age of five.

- **Female octopuses** lay about 50,000 eggs, which they protect as they develop. During this time the mother does not eat, and she dies soon after the eggs hatch.

- **A newly-hatched octopus** is called a larva and it is about one centimetre long.

- **Like other octopuses**, this species has excellent eyesight.

▶ *This giant Pacific octopus is a powerful predator. It hunts mostly at night, prowling close to the sea bed for shelled animals such as crabs and lobsters.*

DID YOU KNOW?

The giant Pacific octopus is one of the most intelligent invertebrates. It can watch and learn how to solve simple problems.

Whelks, sea slugs and topshells

- **Murexes, sea hares, abalones**, cone shells, winkles, whelks and topshells are all types of shelled mollusc.

- **They are gastropods** and live in the seas and oceans, especially in shallow water.

- **Gastropods have** a large, muscular 'foot', a head with tentacles, eyes and a radula (toothed tongue) for feeding.

- **Limpets attach themselves** firmly to rocky coasts so they can withstand the battering of waves and wind. They can survive underwater, and in air when the tide goes out.

- **Whelks, winkles and abalones** are gastropods that are an important source of food for humans. Common whelks feed on bivalve molluscs.

- **Sea slugs are** shell-less gastropods, and are also called nudibranchs.

▶ The colourful shell of a painted topshell mollusc provides the soft-bodied animal inside with protection from predators. The shell also stops the animal drying out between high tide and low tide.

▲ Sea slugs are most common in warm waters, especially around coral reefs, although some species are able to survive in cold Antarctic waters.

Most sea slugs are extremely colourful. Their coloured, patterned skin warns other animals that they are toxic.

Murexes drill a hole into another mollusc's shell to reach the soft body parts inside.

Some species of murex were used in Roman times to create a purple dye that was so rare it could only be used to colour the clothes of the wealthiest people.

Top shells are often delicately coloured and patterned with spiral lines. They mostly feed on algae.

Heteropods are sea snails that lose their shells when they become adults. Unlike most gastropods they float or swim in warm waters. They have two large eyes and once they have found their prey they attack using their radula.

307

Cockles and mussels

- **Cockles and mussels** belong to a group of invertebrates called bivalves, which includes oysters, clams, scallops and razorshells.

- **All bivalves have two shells** that are joined by a hinge. The soft-bodied animal lives inside.

- **Most bivalves feed** by using a tube called a siphon to draw water over their gills. Food particles are trapped in the sticky, hairy gills and sent to the mouth.

▼ Over time, giant clams become a home to seaweeds and marine animals that settle on the huge shells. When the shells are open the fleshy mantle is visible. Algae live in the mantle and provide the animal with food.

◀ A cockle secures itself to the sea bed and removes food from the water as currents pass over it. Most cockles have very thick, ridged shells that can cope with the strong buffeting action of waves at a shore.

🐾 **Cockles burrow in sand** and mud on the seashore. Mussels cling to rocks and breakwaters between the high and low tide marks.

🐾 **Oysters and some other molluscs** line their shells with a hard, shiny, silvery white substance called nacre.

🐾 **When a lump of grit** gets into an oyster shell, it is gradually covered in a ball of nacre, making a pearl.

🐾 **The best pearls come** from the Pinctada pearl oysters, in the Pacific Ocean. The world's biggest pearl was 24 cm across and weighed 6.4 kg. It came from a giant clam.

🐾 **Scallops can swim away** from danger by opening and shutting their shells rapidly to pump out water. However, most bivalves escape danger by shutting themselves up inside their shells.

🐾 **Razor clams** live in deep, vertical burrows in sandy sediments.

🐾 **The largest bivalves** measure up to one metre across. Giant clams live in warm, clean shallow seas especially on coral reefs. Tiny green algae live on their shells and provide the clams with food.

Arthropods

- **Arthropods are a large group** of animals that evolved in the ancient oceans more than 500 million years ago. Today there are at least 1.2 million species of arthropod in the world, including insects, spiders and crabs.

- **Insects, centipedes**, millipedes, crustaceans and arachnids are all types of arthropod.

- **Arthropods do not have bones**. Instead, they have a thickened skin called an exoskeleton, which is extremely tough and arranged in rigid plates.

- **The exoskeleton's outer layer** – the cuticle – provides an extra layer of protection and stops the animal from drying out.

- **Arthropod bodies are** divided into segments and they have distinct heads with sense organs, such as eyes and antennae.

- **They have pairs of** legs that are jointed so they can bend. Some arthropods walk, some swim and some of them can fly, using one or two sets of wings.

▼ Like many arthropods, grasshoppers have colourful bodies and sensitive antennae on their heads.

- **The first arthropods** lived in the sea, but they evolved to live on land, in freshwater and some developed the ability to fly.

- **Giant dragonflies** that lived about 300 million years ago had a wingspan of 60 cm.

- **An arthropod's rigid** exoskeleton stops it from growing bigger. In order for its body to grow, an arthropod must grow a new exoskeleton and shed its old, smaller one.

- **Young arthropods** often look very different to adults. Some types must go through a big change – a metamorphosis – as they develop into adults.

▶ Widely believed to be one of the strongest animals in the world for its size, a male rhinoceros beetle can bear more than 850 times its own weight. Males use this great strength in battles with their rivals.

Millipedes and centipedes

- **A centipede's body** is divided into 16–177 segments. Most segments bear one pair of legs – so a centipede can have fewer than 100 legs, or many more.

- **Almost all centipedes** are carnivores and hunt insects and worms to eat. They live in or near the soil.

- **The legs on a centipede's** front segments have evolved to become venomous claws, which they use to kill their prey.

- **The largest centipedes** can grow enormous – up to 28 cm long. A giant tropical centipede is big enough to attack frogs and mice, but the smaller types are more dangerous to humans.

- **A millipede's body** is more rounded than a centipede's body. There are two pairs of legs on most of the segments, instead of one.

- **Millipedes eat plants** or rotting matter, so they don't need venomous claws to attack prey.

- **When they are under attack**, millipedes roll themselves up into a coil. Pill millipedes roll themselves up into a tight ball.

- **Centipedes are found** all over the world, especially in warm places. Millipedes are most common in the northern hemisphere where they live in soil and in leaf litter. They are good at burrowing.

- **A millipede can have up** to 750 legs but unlike centipedes, which can often run very fast, they tend to move slowly.

◄ The giant Africpoctoan millipede is one of the largest myriapods (the invertebrate group that includes millipedes and centipedes). The largest specimen ever recorded was 38.7 cm long and had 256 legs.

Crustaceans

- **A crustacean is an arthropod** with a tough, 'crusty' exoskeleton, two pairs of antennae and eyes on stalks.

- **Crabs, lobsters, shrimps**, barnacles and spider crabs are all types of crustacean.

- **Most are predators** that have strong body parts that they use for grabbing, crushing and ripping at their prey. Others take small particles of food out of the water.

- **Most crustaceans** live in the sea or freshwater.

- **Woodlice are land-living** crustaceans. They live in damp places and they feed on dead or rotting plants and animals.

▼ A crab's tough exoskeleton is called a carapace and it is strengthened with calcium carbonate. Male and female crabs often look very different, and some types of crab must migrate to find a mate.

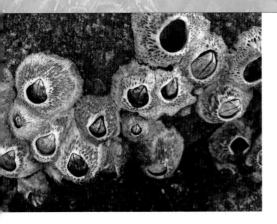

◄ Barnacles attach themselves to rocks, boats and even other animals, such as whales. They have very tough exoskeletons that are made up of plates.

Spider crabs have triangle-shaped bodies and long spindly legs. They often cover their bodies with bits of seaweed or broken shells so they are well-camouflaged on the sea bed.

The largest arthropod is the Japanese spider crab. Its body measures up to 50 cm across and it has a legspan of over 4 m.

Copepods are small crustaceans that swim in the open ocean. They are an important source of food for other marine animals.

A barnacle feeds by extending special body parts, called cirri, into the water and catching tiny animals or plants that swim by.

Water fleas use their antennae like little oars to move through the water. They live in rivers, lakes and ponds.

Beach hoppers live by the coast, especially in piles of rotting seaweed. They jump to escape from predators.

Goose barnacles have long stalks that they use to attach themselves to the sea bed. They are found all over the oceans, even in deep water. They grow up to 80 cm long.

315

Crabs and lobsters

◄ *A lobster uses its large, thick tail to swim and escape from danger at speed. Newly hatched lobsters are kept under their mother's tail until they are big enough to swim away.*

Crabs, lobsters and prawns belong to a huge group of crustaceans that includes more than 38,000 species.

They usually have strong, colourful exoskeletons, eyes on stalks and a pair of legs that work like pincers or claws to grab.

Fiddler crabs are common in warm places, especially coastal habitats, such as sandy beaches and mangrove swamps.

Male fiddler crabs have one claw that is much bigger than the other one, and they use it to attract females or to scare other males away.

Mantis shrimps have excellent eyesight and lightning-quick reactions. They hit both predators and prey with a club-like claw. When they strike a bubble of air is created that is powerful enough to stun prey.

Hermit crabs protect the soft parts of their bodies by living inside the empty shells of sea snails.

- **Crabs and lobsters** are decapods – they have ten legs. The first pair are often strong pincers, used to tear food.

- **One of a lobster's claws** usually has blunt ends for crushing victims. The other has sharp teeth for cutting.

- **The world's largest land crustacean** is the coconut crab. Its legspan measures up to one metre, which helps it climb coconut trees to feed. They are also known as robber crabs, because they steal food whenever they can.

- **American spiny lobsters** migrate hundreds of kilometres, clinging to each others' tails in a long line.

- **Decorator crabs camouflage** themselves by piling sponges and seaweed over their bodies. Hundreds of tiny hooks fix their 'decoration' in place.

▶ *A peacock mantis shrimp measures 5–12 cm and has one of the most complex eye structures in the world. It is able to see a far wider range of colours than humans.*

317

Horseshoe crabs

- **Horseshoe crabs** are arthropods that live in shallow water and on sandy beaches along the Atlantic coast of America, from Canada to Mexico, and parts of Southeast Asia.

- **These arthropods** are not crustaceans and they are more closely related to spiders than to the crab and lobster family.

- **They are often called** 'living fossils' because they have survived, almost unchanged, for about 200 million years.

- **The body is horseshoe-shaped** and is usually 30–60 cm wide. It is protected by a brown exoskeleton that bears five pairs of walking legs and a long, slender tail.

- **A horseshoe crab** has ten eyes in total. Two of these are compound eyes – a type of eye found in insects – but there are eight other very simple 'eyes' that can detect light, including one on its tail.

- **Horseshoe crab females** are bigger than males.

▶ As a horseshoe crab moves along the beach it burrows into the sand and mud, feeling for worms or other prey. It uses its front limbs to grab hold of animals and transfer them to its mouth.

- **Horseshoe crabs** burrow into the sandy sea bed to find food to eat. They hunt other marine animals such as molluscs and worms, which they catch with a pair of claws.

- **In the spring**, horseshoe crabs emerge from the sea and clamber onto the sandy shore to mate. They lay their eggs in the sand then return to the sea.

- **Young horseshoe crabs** are called larvae and they spend the first year of their lives living on or near the shore. As they grow, they move into deeper water.

DID YOU KNOW?

A horseshoe crab uses its skinny spiny tail to turn itself the right way if it gets flipped on to its back.

Arachnids

- **Arachnids are arthropods** with two main body parts and four pairs of legs.

- **The first body part** includes the head and is called a cephalothorax. The legs are attached to the cephalothorax.

- **The second body part** is called the abdomen and this contains the animal's organs for breathing, reproducing and digesting food.

- **Spiders, scorpions, solpugids**, ticks and mites are all types of arachnid.

- **Most arachnids** live on land, although the water spider has evolved to survive in ponds and lakes.

- **Unlike other arachnids**, spiders make silk. They have fangs that are used to inject venom into their prey, or when the spider needs to defend itself.

▶ Tarantulas are large spiders that live in warm places, especially tropical forests. There are about 1000 species, including the red-kneed tarantula of Mexico. Tarantulas have bristles all over their bodies but their bites are rarely venomous.

▲ Solpugids are also known as camel spiders, sun spiders or wind scorpions. They have four pairs of legs – what appears to be a pair of legs by the mouth are sensory feelers.

- **There are about** 42,000 species of spider and they are found in most parts of the world. They are all hunters, and in turn they are eaten by amphibians, reptiles and birds.

- **Vinegaroons are arachnids** with enormous pinching claws. They squirt acid over attackers.

- **Ticks are bloodsuckers** that attach themselves to other animals. They use their mouthparts to dig a hole into their victim, and suck up blood until their bodies swell.

- **Ticks spread diseases** between animals when they feed.

- **Solpugids have huge mouthparts** for mashing their victims into pieces. They live in hot places, and burrow beneath stones to rest during the day.

321

Spiders

- **Spiders are scurrying creatures** which, unlike insects, have eight legs not six, and bodies with two parts not three.

- **They belong to a group** of 103,000 species called arachnids, which also includes scorpions, mites and ticks.

- **Spiders are predators** and most of them feed mainly on insects. Despite their name, bird-eating spiders rarely eat birds, preferring lizards and small rodents such as mice.

- **About half of all spiders** catch their prey by weaving sticky, silken nets called webs. Some webs are simple tubes in holes. Others, called orb webs, are elaborate and round.

- **The Australian trapdoor spider** ambushes its prey from a burrow with a camouflaged entrance flap.

- **The bites of black widow**, redback and funnelweb spiders are so poisonous they can kill humans. Only about 30 of the 42,000 different kinds of spider are dangerous to people.

- **Jumping spiders** have two pairs of huge eyes and superb eyesight. They leap onto their prey and sink their venomous fangs into them.

◄ A jumping spider uses its large eyes to calculate the distance to its prey. It uses its smaller eyes to sense motion. It uses all of this information to land by its prey.

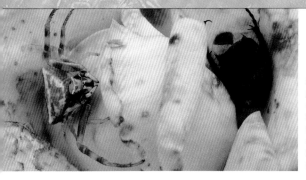

◄ A pink crab spider lurks among the pink petals of a flower so it can leap upon insects visiting the flower to collect its sugary nectar. There are more than 2000 species of crab spider.

🐾 **When crab spiders feed** they suck out their prey's insides, so the insect they have devoured looks almost untouched once they have finished their meal.

🐾 **Only one type** of spider is vegetarian – it is called the *Bagheera kiplingi* and feeds on sweet parts of an acacia tree.

🐾 **Golden wheel spiders** do somersaults as they roll down the sand dunes of their desert home. As they flip and cartwheel along, these arachnids can reach 2 m/sec.

🐾 **Spiders can be divided** into two groups: those that hunt their prey and those that catch or trap it.

DID YOU KNOW?

Black widow spiders are so called because the females often eat their mates after mating.

🐾 **Spiders that hunt** their prey are called 'wandering spiders' and they are often more dangerous to humans.

🐾 **Spitting spiders** fire a jet of sticky poison at their prey.

🐾 **Crab spiders ambush** their prey. Many crab spiders are perfectly camouflaged, and even match the bright colours of flowers where they hide in wait.

Silk, webs and traps

🐾 **Spider silk is made** from protein in special silk glands at the tip of the animal's abdomen. It is unlike any other substance on Earth.

🐾 **As the silk** leaves a spider's body it turns from liquid to solid and is shaped into long, strong, stretchy threads.

🐾 **Silk threads** can stretch up to six times their length before snapping.

🐾 **A spider can make** different kinds of silk to suit the job it must do. Strong, dry silk is best for attaching a web to trees or the ground. Wet, sticky silk is better for trapping insects.

🐾 **Spiders use silk** to wrap their eggs up into a little parcel called a cocoon. This keeps the eggs safe and dry while the little spiderlings grow inside.

🐾 **Orb-web spiders** use their silk to weave complex webs in just 30 minutes.

🐾 **Once the web is completed** the spider hides, touching its silken threads so it can feel when prey becomes trapped.

▶ *Building a web is instinctive; orb-weaving spiders do not learn how to do it but are born with the ability.*

1. The bridge thread

2. A frame is constructed

▶ *Many spiders that do not build webs still use silk to construct silk-lined burrows where they can hide during the day.*

- **Trapdoor spiders** dig a burrow and line it with silk. They make a 'trapdoor' over the top with silk and hide within. When an insect walks nearby the spider leaps out from its burrow and grabs its prey.

- **Spitting spiders** spit a mixture of venom and glue at their prey.

- **Funnel web spiders** can be deadly to humans. They build burrows that are lined with silk and leap out to catch animals that pass nearby.

3. Radial threads are added

4. A first spiral is spun

5. A second, sticky spiral is added

325

Scorpions

- **Scorpions are the oldest members** of the arachnid family.

- **The earliest scorpions** lived in water, but today all scorpions live on land and they are most common in hot, dry habitats.

▼ There are about 1500 species of scorpion, of which about 650 are buthids. A female gives birth to up to 100 young at a time.

- **A scorpion's body** is long, slender and flat enough to squeeze beneath rocks and burrow into the sand or soil.

- **There is a pair of large claws** at the front of the body, and a long tail with a venomous sting at the end.

DID YOU KNOW?

A hungry scorpion mother may give birth and then start to eat her own babies.

- **When a scorpion** attacks its prey it grabs it with its claws and curls its long tail over its head to inject venom into the helpless victim.

- **The largest scorpion** ever found measured nearly 30 cm long.

- **Female scorpions** do not lay eggs. They give birth to live young, and some species carry their babies on their back until they are able to look after themselves.

- **There are two families** of scorpion: buthids and scorpionids.

- **Buthids are smallest** and they live worldwide. Scorpionids are larger but they are less deadly than smaller buthids.

- **The death stalker scorpion** lives in parts of Africa and the Middle East. It is the world's most venomous scorpion but it lives in places where there are few humans.

- **Scorpions eat insects**. When food is scarce a scorpion can survive a whole year after eating just one insect.

- **A scorpion glows** under ultra-violet light, but scientists don't know why they have developed this strange feature.

Insects

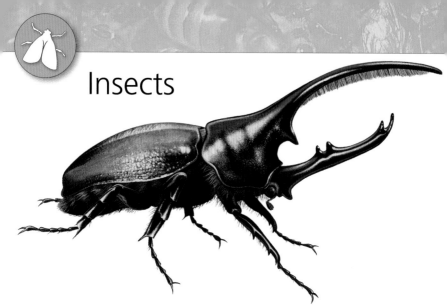

▲ *Like other insects, the adult Hercules beetle has three pairs of legs. Its wings are hidden beneath wing covers. A male's 'horns' can grow longer than its entire body and are used in fights with other males.*

The insects are a massive group of highly successful animals that live in almost every habitat on Earth.

Although most insects live on land or in freshwater some species survive in ocean water.

Insects are the only invertebrates that can fly.

Beetles, flies, bees, butterflies and grasshoppers are all types of insect. They have three body parts: a head, a thorax and an abdomen.

Insects have three pairs of legs and some of them have wings.

An insect's antennae are good at sensing the animal's environment. They are used to touch, taste, listen and smell.

- **Many insects have compound eyes** that are made up of many tiny lenses.

- **More than one million** species of insect have been discovered so far, but scientists believe there could be millions more.

- **Insects often** have complicated life cycles. Most of them lay eggs that hatch into larvae, which often look very different to the adults and live in different habitats.

- **Many insect larvae** live in water, but take to the land when they turn into adults. These aquatic larvae have gills for breathing.

- **An insect's mouthparts** are the right size and shape for its diet. Some have crushing jaws to grab and crunch tough-skinned invertebrates; others have straw-like mouthparts for sucking up the sweet nectar in a flower.

▶ *The giant weta is one of the heaviest insects in the world. Once common in New Zealand, this bizarre insect now lives solely on a few small islands.*

Fleas and lice

- **Fleas and lice** are insects that live their lives as parasites.

- **Fleas feed on blood**. They live on the outside of an animal's body and use their piercing mouthparts to suck.

- **There are about** 2400 species of flea but they all look similar. Fleas are tiny, with flattened bodies and long legs that they use to leap. Fleas don't have wings.

- **Some fleas only live** on one type of animal, but others are more adaptable and can take blood from many types of host.

- **Flea eggs hatch** into tiny larvae that do not live on a host. They often live in birds' nests, animal burrows, or pets' bedding. When they turn into adults the fleas wait until they sense a host animal is nearby, then jump onto it.

- **Rat fleas** carried the bubonic plague – a terrible disease that caused the deaths of millions of people in Medieval Europe.

- **Lice are wingless** with flattened bodies.

- **The shape** of a louse's body is perfect for scampering through hair and fur. They use their clawed legs to grip onto strands of hair.

- **A louse feeds** on blood and their hosts are birds or mammals. Human lice live on the head and glue their eggs to strands of hair. The eggs are white and shiny and are called nits.

- **Bird lice feed** on blood, but they also eat away at feathers and damage a bird's skin, making it more likely to get other infections.

▼ *Fleas are described as hematophagous, which means they live on a diet of blood. Their bodies are surprisingly tough, which is why they often survive scratching, squeezing and squashing by their host.*

DID YOU KNOW?

Fleas have little elastic pads at the base of their legs, which catapult them into the air.

Cockroaches

Cockroaches are flat-bodied insects that scavenge food and eat anything edible they can find, including animal dung.

▼ *Madagascar hissing cockroaches have an unusual method of defence. They force air out of their breathing tubes to create a hissing sound that frightens predators.*

- **They live all over the world**, especially in tropical places. They prefer cool, dark and damp habitats and many types are found in tropical forests where they live in leaf litter.

- **Cockroaches have a** reputation as pests, but less than one percent of all species spreads disease.

- **The smallest cockroach** is less than 3 mm long and lives inside ant nests. The Australian rhinoceros cockroach measures 8 cm in length.

- **Although these insects** are land-living they are able to survive in water. They often run towards water when they are under attack.

- **The oldest cockroach fossil** is more than 300 million years old, which means that cockroaches existed long before the dinosaurs.

- **A cockroach is extremely sensitive** to vibrations and will disappear in seconds when it is disturbed. Their flat shape allows them to hide in the smallest spaces.

- **Females lay 14–30 eggs**, which are stored in a tough case called an ootheca.

- **Some females leave** the ootheca in a safe place where the eggs develop on their own. The females of other species carry their ootheca with them, so they can protect it from predators.

- **Some cockroaches** give birth to live young. The females keep the ootheca within their bodies, and the young hatch there.

- **A young cockroach** is called a nymph and it may have to moult (shed its exoskeleton) up to 13 times as it reaches maturity.

Termites

For a long time, scientists thought that termites were closely related to ants because they look and live quite similarly. Now it is known that termites are cockroaches that evolved to be able to eat and digest wood.

Termites have saw-toothed jaws for cutting through the tough fibres that make wood such a strong material.

A termite's body is small, soft and pale. They are usually wingless, with short hair-like antennae. They live in large groups called colonies that contain up to 10,000 insects, and build big nests.

The termites in a colony have different jobs to do: a king and queen produce all the eggs, soldiers defend the nest and workers build the nest and provide food.

▶ Worker termites care for the young, which are called nymphs or larvae. Only some of the young will go on to grow wings.

🐾 **Termites make nests** underground, which sometimes grow as mounds above the ground, reaching several metres in height. The tallest termite mounds are found in Africa, where one mound measured 12.8 m tall.

🐾 **A queen termite** measures up to 14 cm long and is like a giant egg-making machine. She can lay up to 30,000 eggs a day.

🐾 **There are nearly** 3000 species of termite and they are particularly common in hot, tropical places. There can be up to 10,000 termites in just one square metre of rainforest soil.

🐾 **A termite nest** is built with tunnels and channels that encourage the flow of air. This means the temperature stays stable and the air does not get too moist.

🐾 **They are probably** the most important animal group involved in removing dead and rotting plants. They help to improve soil, so new plants can grow well.

🐾 **Termites can do great damage** to buildings, fences and crops, so they are considered a pest in many human habitats.

▶ *Mound-building termites are common in Africa, Australia and South America. Much of the nest is actually built underground.*

335

Flies

◀ Like many insects, flies have large eyes that are made up of many tiny lenses. Each lens 'sees' a separate image. This type of eye is called a compound eye.

- **Flies are one** of the biggest groups of insects, common nearly everywhere. There are 150,000 species.

- **Most flies are agile**, acrobatic fliers. They can hover, and fly backwards, sideways and upside down. Some can even take off and land while upside down.

- **Flies include bluebottles**, black flies, gnats, horseflies, midges, mosquitoes and tsetse flies.

- **The eyes of the stalk-eyed fly** are at the end of long stalks, much wider than its body. Males compete to see who has the longest eye stalks.

- **Flies suck up** their food – typically sap from rotting plants. Houseflies often suck liquids from manure, while blowflies drink juices from rotting meat.

- **Some flies have** mouthparts that suck. Others have a pad that dissolves their food and soaks it up like a sponge.

- **The larvae (young)** of flies are called maggots, and they are tiny, white, wriggling and tube-shaped.

- **Flies mimic (copy)** other insects. There are wasp-flies, drone-flies, ant-flies, moth-flies and beetle-flies.

- **Many species of fly** are carriers of dangerous diseases. When a fly bites or makes contact, it can infect people with some of the germs it carries – especially the flies that suck blood. Mosquitoes spread malaria, and tsetse flies spread sleeping sickness.

◄ Stalk-eyed flies are most common in Africa and Southeast Asia. Both males and females have the unusual head shape.

Mosquitoes

- **Mosquitoes are flies** that spread killer diseases including malaria, dengue fever, elephantiasis, yellow fever and many others.

- **A male mosquito** always feeds on nectar and other plant juices, but females need a meal of blood to lay their eggs.

- **All mosquitoes lay** their eggs in water. The eggs hatch within a few days and the larvae stay in the water, hanging from the surface so their breathing tubes can reach the air.

- **The larvae** shed their skins as they grow, and they feed on small animals in the water.

- **When it is time** to change into an adult a larva forms a pupa, where its body takes on the adult shape.

- **A female can find** a human victim by sensing their breath, their body heat and smells, especially the smell of sweat.

- **Once she has landed**, the female forces two long tubes, which make up her mouthparts into the flesh. Chemicals that stop the blood from clotting flow down one tube, and blood is sucked up through the other one.

- **As a mosquito feeds**, the microbes that spread disease pass through her mouthparts into her victim.

- **Asian tiger mosquitoes** have striking black and white bodies. They spread diseases to humans, but also infect cats and dogs.

DID YOU KNOW?

A blood-sucking mosquito feeds for about 4 minutes at a time. It sucks so hard its victim's tiny blood vessels may collapse.

🐾 **Midges look very similar** to mosquitoes, but they are not able to bite because they don't have working mouthparts. They spend most of their lives as larvae in water, only living for a few weeks as adults because they cannot eat.

▼ *A tube-like insect mouthpart is called a proboscis. As a female mosquito draws blood into her body her abdomen expands to make room.*

339

Bugs

- **Bugs are insects** that feed by piercing and then sucking up plant and animal juices through long, straw-like mouthparts.

- **There are approximately** 88,000 species of bugs, including aphids, shield bugs and cicadas. They range in size from less than one millimetre to over 11 cm in length.

- **There are two main** groups of bugs. True bugs' front wings have a leathery exterior and thin, see-through tips. Other bugs have one or two pairs of wings that are the same all over.

- **Cicadas are one** of the loudest insects. A cicada's courtship song is a high-pitched screech, produced by clicking lid-like structures on its abdomen.

- **Assassin bugs stab prey** with their feeding tube and inject a paralyzing poison. The poison turns the insides of the prey into a liquid. The bug sucks this out, leaving a dry, empty husk behind.

- **Shield bugs are** sometimes called stink bugs. They produce a horrible smell when they are handled, which deters predators.

- **Pond skaters**, or water striders, are lightweight bugs that can walk on the surface of the water without sinking. Their long legs spread out their weight so the water's surface dips down under their feet but does not break.

- **Thorn bugs** have a sharp spine growing over the wings, making them look like plant thorns.

- **Backswimmers swim** through the water upside down, carrying a supply of air in a cage of hairs under their bodies. They can stay underwater for several minutes, to feed on small fish and tadpoles.

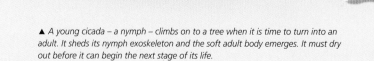

▲ *A young cicada – a nymph – climbs on to a tree when it is time to turn into an adult. It sheds its nymph exoskeleton and the soft adult body emerges. It must dry out before it can begin the next stage of its life.*

Beetles

- **At least 370,000** species of beetle have been identified. They live everywhere on Earth, apart from in the oceans.

- **Unlike other insects**, adult beetles have a pair of thick, hard, front wings called elytra. These form an armour-like casing over the beetle's body.

▼ The bombardier beetle's bold colouring warns other animals to stay away, or risk being sprayed by acid.

DID YOU KNOW?

The Arctic beetle feeds on rotting wood and can survive in temperatures below –60°C.

- **The Goliath beetle** of Africa is the heaviest flying insect, weighing over 100 g and growing to as much as 15 cm in length.

- **A click beetle** can jump 30 cm into the air to escape or startle predators or to turn itself the right way up. It is named after the loud sound it makes when it jumps.

- **The bombardier beetle** mixes up a cocktail of chemicals inside its body to make a boiling hot spray. It squirts this spray from the end of its abdomen.

- **To protect itself**, the bloody-nosed beetle gives off a bright-red liquid from its mouth. Most predators prefer to leave this strange beetle alone.

- **Great diving beetles** live underwater in ponds and lakes. They breathe from air bubbles that they collect from the surface and store under their elytra (wing cases).

- **Stag beetles have** huge jaws that look like a stag's antlers. Male stag beetles fight with their 'antlers'. Each male tries to lift his rival into the air and smash him to the ground. The winner of the fight gets to mate with the female.

- **Fireflies produce** a special pattern of flashing lights to signal to their mates. The light is made by the beetles mixing chemicals inside their abdomens to cause a reaction that releases light energy.

343

Scarab beetles

- **Scarab beetles** make up an enormous family of beetles with about 30,000 species.

- **They have stout**, rounded bodies and some types are brightly coloured with a metallic sheen.

- **The scarabs are** the heaviest beetles – and some of the biggest insects – alive. The larva of the *megasoma actaeon* is a huge pale grub that weighs as much as two apples.

- **An adult Hercules beetle** reaches 17 cm long.

- **In tests**, it was found that an Australian dung beetle could pull 1141 times its own weight. That is like a human lifting six double-decker buses.

- **Ancient Egyptians** worshipped sacred scarab beetles, which often featured in their art and decorations on tombs and temples.

▶ Rose chafer beetles are common in parts of Europe. Adults feed on flower petals but the larvae eat rotting leaves and help to create garden compost.

- **Scarabs eat a range of food**, from fruit to insects. One type survives by eating the slime left by snails as they slither.

- **Dung beetles are scarabs** that eat dung – animal waste. They eat the dung of large herbivores, such as rhinos and elephants, because the plant matter waste that passes out of their guts still contains nutrients.

- **A dung beetle** finds dung using its keen sense of smell.

- **There are relatively** few scarab beetles in Australia, so farmers import them to remove the dung produced by their cattle.

- **Not all dung beetles** roll dung, some simply crawl inside and start eating.

- **Female dung beetles** lay a single egg in a buried ball of dung. When the larva hatches it stays in the dung, feeding and growing until it reaches adulthood.

- **Precious metal scarabs** have shiny gold or silver bodies. They are found in Central and South America, and no one knows why they have such vivid colouring.

▶ *A dung beetle rolls a pile of dung into a ball, which it pushes with its hind legs to a safe place where it may be buried or eaten immediately.*

Metamorphosis

Insects change as they grow from eggs to adults. For many types of insect the change from juvenile (young insect) to adult is a major change in shape. This change is called a metamorphosis.

Some insect juveniles look similar to the adults. As they grow, they moult their exoskeleton several times as they reach the adult size. This is called an incomplete metamorphosis.

▼ *During metamorphosis a butterfly is called a pupa. The hard case that surrounds the pupa during this change is called a chrysalis. It splits open when it is time for an adult to emerge.*

- **Juvenile insects** that look like the adults, but smaller, are called nymphs.

- **Butterfly and moth** juveniles are called caterpillars and young flies are called maggots.

- **Only adult insects** are able to reproduce and lay eggs. Some adult insects do not eat because they only need to live long enough to reproduce.

- **Juveniles often live** in different habitats to their parents so they are not competing for space or food.

- **Some insect juveniles** look very different to the adults. They moult as they grow, but after the final moult they turn into a pupa. The adult emerges from the pupa. This is a complete metamorphosis.

- **Caterpillars must eat** a huge amount of food and grow quickly to prepare for metamorphosis.

- **When a caterpillar prepares** to pupate it grows a hard case around itself. Inside the case, the insect's body completely changes as it develops three body segments, wings and legs.

- **There are 26 orders of insect**, and only nine of them go through complete metamorphosis. However, these nine orders make up 80 percent of all insects.

- **Changes in temperature** can affect the size, colour and shape of an adult insect that emerges after metamorphosis.

347

Moths

- **With butterflies**, moths make up the Lepidoptera ('scaly wings') group. There are about 170,000 species of Lepidoptera – about 10 percent are butterflies, the rest are moths.

- **The young (larvae)** of moths are called caterpillars. When they are ready to develop into adults they form a pupa, protected by a case called a chrysalis, or a cocoon made from silk. Finally the adult crawls out, dries off and flies away.

- **At rest**, moths spread their wings or fold them flat, while butterflies hold their wings upright. Moths have thread-like or feathery antennae (feelers), while butterfly antennae have clubs on the end.

- **Many moths fly** at dusk or at night. By day, they rest in trees, where they are hard for predators to spot. However, there are also many brightly coloured day-flying moths.

- **Tiger moths** give out high-pitched clicks to warn that they taste bad and so escape being eaten.

- **The biggest moths** are the giant Atlas moth and the Giant Agrippa moth, with wingspans of up to 30 cm.

- **The hornet clearwing moth** looks like a hornet, so birds leave it alone, even though it cannot sting.

- **Hawk moths migrate** long distances. The oleander hawk moth flies from Africa to northern Europe in summer.

- **The caterpillars** of small moths live in seeds, fruit, stems and leaves, eating them from the inside.

- **Big moths' caterpillars** feed on leaves from the outside, chewing chunks out of them.

- **When threatened**, the caterpillar of the puss moth rears up, thrusts its whip-like tail forward and squirts a jet of formic acid from its head end.

▼ The Morgan's sphinx moth is particularly well-known because it is the only insect able to reach the nectar in Darwin's orchids – flowers with very long nectar tubes. The moth's proboscis (mouthpart) is about 30 cm long.

Butterflies

- **Butterflies are insects** with four large wings that feed either on the nectar of flowers or on fruit.

- **The body shape** of a butterfly completely changes between the larval stage and adulthood. Butterfly larvae are called caterpillars. When they are ready to develop into adults, the caterpillars form a pupa, inside a chrysalis.

- **Many butterflies** are brightly coloured and fly by day. They have slim bodies and club-shaped antennae.

- **The biggest butterfly** is the female Queen Alexandra's birdwing of New Guinea, with 28-cm-wide wings. The smallest is the Western pygmy blue.

- **Peacock butterflies** have eye-like markings on their wings, which may startle predators and divert their attention away from the butterfly's real eyes.

◀ The spectacular eyespots of a peacock butterfly startle predators, giving the insect time to escape.

▶ Like many butterflies, the small copper has become more rare in the last century. It prefers warm, dry habitats, especially wastelands, grasslands and heaths.

🐾 **Leaf butterflies look** exactly like a dry, brown leaf when they hold their wings shut. The Indian leaf butterfly even has lines on its wings that look like the veins on a real leaf.

🐾 **Monarch butterflies** are such strong fliers they migrate between North and Central America, covering distances of thousands of kilometres. A few have even crossed the Atlantic Ocean.

🐾 **Most female butterflies** live for only a few weeks, so they have to mate and lay eggs quickly. Most males court them with elaborate flying displays.

🐾 **Every butterfly's caterpillar** has its own chosen food plants – different from the flowers the adult feeds on.

◀ Many butterflies spread their wings but green hairstreaks rest with their wings closed, showing the green metallic undersides. They usually feed on nectar from shrubs such as bramble.

Dragonflies

- **Dragonflies are big** hunting insects with four large transparent wings and long, slender bodies that may be shimmering reds, greens or blues.

- **Dragonflies have 30,000 lenses** in each of their compound eyes, and the sharpest vision of any insect.

- **A dragonfly's enormous eyes** allow it to detect movement easily and spot prey, such as midges, mosquitoes or moths, from up to 12 m away.

- **As it swoops** in on its prey, a dragonfly pulls its legs forwards like a basket to scoop up its victim.

- **Dragonflies often** mate in mid-air, and the male may then stay hanging onto the female until she lays her eggs.

- **Dragonfly eggs** are laid in water or in the stem of a water plant, and hatch in 2–3 weeks.

- **Newly hatched** dragonflies are called nymphs and look like fatter, wingless adults.